Editor
Eric Migliaccio

Managing Editor
Ina Massler Levin, M.A.

Editor-in-Chief
Sharon Coan, M.S. Ed.

Cover Artist
Denise Bauer

Illustrator
Renee Christine Yates

Art Coordinator
Kevin Barnes

Imaging
Rosa C. See
Temo Parra
James Edward Grace

Product Manager
Phil Garcia

Publisher
Mary D. Smith, M.S. Ed.

Nonfiction Strategies

Includes Standards & Benchmarks

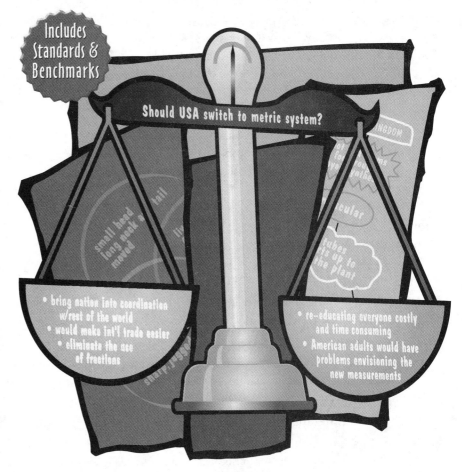

Should USA switch to metric system?

• bring nation into coordination w/rest of the world
• would make int'l trade easier
• eliminate the use of fractions

• re-educating everyone costly and time consuming
• American adults would have problems envisioning the new measurements

Author

Debra J. Housel, M.S. Ed.

Teacher Created Resources

Teacher Created Resources, Inc.
6421 Industry Way
Westminster, CA 92683
www.teachercreated.com

ISBN 13: 978-0-7439-3271-4

©2002 Teacher Created Resources, Inc.
Reprinted, 2007
Made in U.S.A.

Table of Contents

Introduction

The ability to handle nonfiction information effectively has greater importance today than ever before in human history. Over 75 percent of all materials that are written, published, or available in electronic form on the Internet are nonfiction. So much expository text exists that many refer to it as an "information explosion." Clearly your students need instruction that teaches them how to read, write, discuss, research, remember, and listen to information. *Nonfiction Strategies* will help you to prepare them for these prerequisites for success in the 21st century.

Organization of this Book

Mastery of nonfiction comprehension skills comes from regular, meaningful practice over a period of time. The five steps of scaffolded instruction (Blachowicz & Ogle, 2001) provide a guide for teaching any nonfiction skill:

1. Identify and set standards-based goals.

2. Model the learning behavior.

3. Provide guided practice (lead the students through the process).

4. Provide independent practice (gradually release responsibility to the learners).

5. Assess student learning and performance.

Nonfiction Strategies supports all aspects of scaffolded instruction. It contains two correlation charts, eight major strategy sections, and a bibliography. The strategy sections include quick and easy ideas that you can implement in 15 minutes or less, as well as strategies that encompass an entire lesson or unit. Every strategy section includes at least two graphic organizers; the book has a total of 40.

- The **McREL Standards Correlation Chart** identifies specific strategies to meet the standards and related benchmarks for language arts. (Copyright 2000 McREL, Mid-continent Research for Education and Learning, 2250 S. Parker Road, Suite 500, Aurora, CO 80014. Telephone: 303–337–0990.)

- A **Content Area Correlation Chart** lets you check each strategy to see if it is recommended for a specific content area.

- **Preparing Students for Nonfiction** gives ideas and strategies that will develop students' vocabulary, knowledge, and prediction capabilities.

- **Reading Nonfiction** offers techniques for helping students to comprehend what they read in expository texts.

- **Discussing Nonfiction** outlines ways to organize and facilitate effective and thought-provoking whole-group, small-group, and partner discussions. Discussion prompts offer critical-thinking questions so students will grapple with issues using their higher-level thinking skills.

- **Listening to Nonfiction** offers a variety of specific strategies proven to enhance your students' critical-listening skills and ability to glean key information and essential details from lectures, speeches, and audiovisual presentations.

Introduction *(cont.)*

- **Remembering Nonfiction** suggests different research-based techniques to help move information from students' short-term memories into permanent memory storage.

- **Writing Nonfiction** recommends ways to develop your students' ability to write both formal and informal expository pieces.

- **Researching Nonfiction** provides a systematic approach that scaffolds your students' abilities to conduct research and prepare accurate, engaging presentations and written reports.

- **Assessing Students' Nonfiction Comprehension** presents a wealth of ideas for authentically evaluating students' nonfiction understanding. This section takes you beyond the confines of traditional paper-and-pencil objective tests by explaining how to create and use a portfolio system in addition to providing five assessment tools.

- **Resources** list all the journal articles and books cited. These provide primary source information for many of the strategies.

How to Use this Book

The strategies can be used to enrich any unit in any subject. Skim *Nonfiction Strategies* to familiarize yourself with its contents. Then choose a way to use the book most effectively that works for you. Here are some possibilities:

1. Decide which kind of skill(s) your students will need for the particular expository selection. For example, you may choose one strategy from Preparing Students for Nonfiction, another from Reading Nonfiction, and a third from Discussing Nonfiction for the same topic or unit. Check the Content Area Correlation Chart (pages 12–15) to determine if the strategies you've selected are recommended for the subject area. Then refer to the McREL Standards Correlation Chart (pages 5–11) to determine the standard(s) and benchmark(s) your lessons will cover.

2. Determine the standard(s) and benchmark(s) you want to cover in your lesson or unit. Use the McREL Standards Correlation Chart to locate strategies that utilize those skills. Read the strategies over and pick one or more. Refer to the Content Area Correlation Chart to determine if the strategies you have selected are recommended for the subject area.

3. If you are interested in using a specific strategy, refer to the Content Area Correlation Chart to determine if those you have selected are recommended for the subject area. Then cross reference the strategy in the McREL Standards Correlation Chart to determine the standard(s) and benchmark(s) your lessons will cover.

McREL Standards Correlation

McREL Standards are in bold print. Benchmarks are in regular print.

Standards & Benchmarks	Strategy Name	Page(s)
Language Arts (Writing)		
Demonstrates competence in the general skills and strategies of the writing process.	(*See Writing Nonfiction section.*) Written summation/retelling scoring guide	120–137 167
Evaluates own and other's writing	• Editing conferences • Peer editing • Praise-question-polish	122 122 122
Writes with a logical sequence of events	• Stairstep sequencer • Experience writing	58 123
Writes essays that show awareness of intended audience	• Dissecting essay questions • Creative nonfiction writing: RAFT	134 125
Writes essays that convey an intended purpose	• Essay templates • Dissecting essay questions • Creative nonfiction writing: RAFT	134 134 125
Writes expository compositions	• Key sentences • Dissecting essay questions • Essay templates • Vocabulary into essay	126 134 134 162
Uses style and structure appropriate for specific audiences and purposes	• Writing in response to text • Creative nonfiction writing: RAFT	124 125
Writes biographical sketches	• Biopoems • Key sentences	130 126
Writes persuasive compositions	• Defend your stance • Letters to the editor • Opinion and support diamond	135 135 136
Writes compositions that speculate on problems and solutions	• Defend your stance • Weighing the choices • Opinion and support diamond	135 96 136
Writes letters	• Letters to the editor • Creative nonfiction writing: RAFT • Doing primary-source research	135 125 142
Writes in response to literature	• Writing in response to text • Creative nonfiction writing: RAFT	124 125
Demonstrates competence in the stylistic and rhetorical aspects of writing.		
Uses descriptive language that clarifies and enhances ideas	• Life-experiences vocabulary • A-B-C summary • Using active verbs • Word association	103 104 121 17

McREL Standards Correlation *(cont.)*

Standards & Benchmarks.	Strategy Name	Page(s)
Uses paragraph form in writing	• Learning logs	120
	• Key sentences	126
	• Visual syntetics	71
	• Vocabulary into essay	162
	• Concept wheel	66
	• Magnet summaries	128
Uses a variety of sentence structures	• Formulating leads and conclusions	121
	• Using active verbs	121
	• Summarizing	104
	• Internalized response	102
	• Home-school folder	108
Uses grammatical and mechanical conventions in written compositions.		
Uses simple and compound sentences in written compositions	• Formulating leads and conclusions	121
	• Using active verbs	121
Uses standard format in written compositions, including footnotes and reference citations	• Written reports	153
	• Citing sources	153
Gathers and uses information for research purposes.	• *(See Researching Nonfiction section.)*	138–153
	• Research and written report scoring guide	169
	• Research and presentation scoring guide	170
Uses a variety of strategies to identify topics to investigate	• Inquiry-based research	139
	• The research process	140
	• Helping students establish research questions	139
Uses key words, indexes, cross-references, and letters on volumes to find information	• Using the library for research	145
	• Knowing where to look for answers	144
	• Using a computer for research	145
Uses multiple representations of information (maps, charts, photos) to find information	• Time lines	60
	• SQ3R	104
	• You're in the picture	24
	• Strategic questioning	37
Uses graphic organizers to gather and record information	• Sum it up chart	146
	• Inquiry chart	148
	• K-W-L chart	150
	• Herringbone	164
Compiles information into written reports or summaries	• Sustained summary writing	129
	• Magnet summaries	128
	• Summary frame	130
	• Summary grid	81
	• Stairstep sequencer	58
Gathers data for research from interviews	• Writing about a past event	123
	• Experience writing	123
	• Surveys	142
	• Community of learners	143

McREL Standards Correlation *(cont.)*

Standards & Benchmarks	Strategy Name	Page(s)
Uses a variety of resource materials to gather information	• Using the library for research • Using the computer for research	145 145
Determines the appropriateness of an information source for a research topic	• Considering the source • Evaluating sources	98 144
Organizes information and ideas from multiple sources in systematic ways	• Time lines • Informal notes outline • Key word notes	60 112 114
Writes research papers	• Written reports • Creating graphics • Jackdaws • Guided imagery	153 143 152 152
Language Arts (Reading)		
Demonstrates competence in the skills and strategies of the reading process	*(See Reading Nonfiction section.)*	40–69
Creates mental images from pictures and print	• Envisioning text while reading • Key word imaging • Visualizing while listening • Text response centers	50 103 84 115
Uses pictures and captions to aid comprehension and to make predictions about content	• A picture is worth a thousand words • You're in the picture • SQ3R	17 24 104
Previews text	• Directed reading-thinking activity • Turning headings into questions • Strategic questioning	40 45 37
Establishes a purpose for reading	• Focus frame • Selective reading guide • Knowledge tier • Advanced organizer • Turning headings into questions	34 41 118 36 45
Makes, confirms, and revises predictions about what will be found in a text	• Focus frame • Cloze • Read alouds • Think alouds • ReQuest	34 156 16 36 44
Monitors own reading strategies and makes modifications as needed	• Self-monitoring reading strategy • Judicious highlighting	42 103
Generates interesting questions to be answered while reading	• Asking questions before, during, and after reading • Knowledge tier • Questions on trial • What I want to know is… • Focus frame	43 118 45 46 34

McREL Standards Correlation *(cont.)*

Standards & Benchmarks	Strategy Name	Page(s)
Uses a variety of strategies to define and extend understanding of word meaning	• Important word parts in English	29
	• Word trees	30
	• Unlock the meanings of new words	28
	• Life experiences vocabulary	103
	• Introducing new vocabulary	28
Uses specific strategies to clear up confusing parts of a text	• Self-monitoring reading strategy	42
	• Think-alouds	36
	• Asking questions before, during, and after reading	43
Identifies the author's purpose	• Thinking guide	32
	• Considering the source	98
	• Examining the author's motivation	68
Identifies specific devices an author uses to accomplish his or her purpose	• Recognizing persuasive language	88
	• Differentiating between facts and opinions	74
	• Defend your stance	135
	• Discussion prompts	74
	• Voice	86
Reflects on what has been learned after reading and formulates, ideas, opinions, and personal responses to texts	• Internalized response	102
	• Reaction guide	89
	• Venn diagram (2-circle)	61
	• Venn diagram (3-circle)	62
	• Opinion and support diamond	136
	• Quick review	
	• Scattergories	106
Demonstrates competence in the general skills and strategies for reading a variety of informational texts.		
Applies reading skills and strategies to a variety of informational books	• Essential questions	64
	• Concept wheel	66
	• Herringbone	164
	• Judicious highlighting	103
	• Concept organization	39
Understands the main idea of expository information	• Finding the main idea and supporting details	51
	• GIST: Finding the main idea	51
	• Main idea: equation	160
	• Main idea: Greek temple	54
	• Main idea: pyramid	52
	• Main idea: balancing bar	94
Summarizes information found in texts in his or her own words	• Telegraph summary	129
	• Summarizing	104
	• A-B-C summary	104
	• Bare bones summary	110
	• Paraphrasing a song	120
	• Sum-it-up chart	146
	• Summary grid	81

McREL Standards Correlation *(cont.)*

Standards & Benchmarks	Strategy Name	Page(s)
Knows the defining characteristics of a variety of informational texts	• Distinguishing between fiction and nonfiction • Text structure • What are the features of nonfiction works? • Understanding and using parts of a textbook • Knowing where to look for answers	16 57 80 17 144
Uses text organizers to determine the main ideas and to locate information in a text	• Essential questions • Concept wheel • Herringbone • Text structure • Signal words • Teaching inferential skills	64 66 164 57 56 56
Identified and uses the various parts of a book to locate information	• Understanding and using parts of a textbook • Knowing where to look for answers • What are the features of nonfiction works? • Evaluating sources	17 144 80 144
Uses prior knowledge and experience to understand and respond to new information	• Schema activation plan • Anticipation guide • Knowledge rating • Analogy as an introduction • Question-answer relationships • Quick writes • Levels of comprehension guide	24 26 22 18 48 18 91
Identified the author's viewpoint in an informational text	• Examining the author's motivation • Thinking guide • Discussion prompts • Recognizing persuasive language • Listening to different points of view	68 32 74 88 86
Summarizes complex, explicit hierarchic structures in informational texts	• Hierarchy array • Guided reading procedure • Vocabulary into essay • Concept organization	23 132 162 39
Identifies information-organizing strategies that are personally most useful	• Independent mind maps • Key word notes • Informal notes outline • Five fingers • Acronyms • Songs and rhymes • Judicious highlighting • SQ3R	101 114 112 102 101 101 103 104

McREL Standards Correlation *(cont.)*

Standards & Benchmarks	Strategy Name	Page(s)
Uses new information to adjust and extend personal knowledge base	• Directed expository reading • Summary frame • Categorizing • List-group-label • Semantic matrix	81 130 18 19 20
Identifies techniques used to convey viewpoint	• Recognizing persuasive language • Taking a stand • Defend your stance • Seeing it from both sides • Discussion prompts	88 71 135 71 74
Seeks peer help to understand information	• Self-monitoring reading strategy • Free association	42 38
Draws conclusions and makes inferences based on explicit and implicit information in texts	• Teaching inferential skills • Signal words • Text structure • Visual syntetics • Analogy as an introduction	56 56 57 71 18
Differentiates between fact and opinion in informational texts	• Differentiating between facts and opinions • Discussing facts and opinions	88 74
Language Arts (Listening and Speaking)		
Demonstrates competence in speaking and listening as tools for learning	*(See Discussing Nonfiction section.)* Oral summation/retelling scoring guide *(See Listening to Nonfiction section.)*	70–83 166 84–100
Makes contributions in class and group discussions	• Jigsaw • Student achievement teams • Collaborative strategic reading • Discussion prompts • Computer simulations • Possible sentences	78 77 79 74 80 90
Asks questions of teacher and others	• Questioning the author • Enabling questions • Cooperative listening • Question exchange • Circle of knowledge review	72 84 99 105 105
Responds to questions and comments	• Why? Pie • Discussion prompts • Levels of comprehension guide • Film discussion • Question exchange	82 74 91 86 105

McREL Standards Correlation *(cont.)*

Standards & Benchmarks	Strategy Name	Page(s)
Listens to classmates and adults	• Readers guild • Brainstorming carousel • Listening guide • Listen-read-discuss • Class observer	79 76 90 87 70
Organizes ideas for oral presentations	• Taking a stand • Roundtable alphabet • Collaborative listening/viewing guide • Guided imagery	71 116 152
Plays a variety of roles in small group discussions	• Roundtable discussion • Interactive reading guide • Summary grid • Collaborative strategic reading	77 80 81 79
Listens in order to understand a speaker's topic, purpose, and perspective	• Discussing emotions • Discussing facts and opinions • Voice • Listening to different points of view • Examining the author's motivation • Considering the source • Directed listening-thinking activity	70 86 86 68 98 90
Conveys a clear main point when speaking to others and stays on topic being discussed	• You are there • Taking a stand • Discussion prompts	102 71 74
Presents prepared reports to the class	• Class note taker • Written reports	87 153
Identifies strategies used by speakers in oral presentations (e.g. persuasive techniques, the use of fact or opinion)	• Seeing it from both sides • Taking a stand • Listening to different points of view	71 71 80

Standards and benchmarks used by permission of McREL. Kendall, John S., and Marzano, Robert J. (1997) *Content Knowledge: A Compendium of Standards and Benchmarks for K–12 Education* (2nd Edition). Aurora, CO. McREL.

Content Area Correlation Chart

This alphabetical list shows you in which content area(s) each strategy works well.

Strategy Name	Page(s)	Social Studies	Science	Math
A picture is worth a thousand words	17	✓		
A-B-C summary	104	✓	✓	✓
Acronyms	101	✓	✓	
Advanced organizer	36	✓	✓	
Analogy as an introduction	18	✓	✓	
Anticipation guide	26	✓	✓	
Asking questions before, during, and after reading	43	✓	✓	✓
Bare bones summary	110	✓	✓	
Biopoems	130	✓		
Brainstorming carousel	76	✓		
Categorizing	18	✓	✓	✓
Circle of knowledge review	105	✓	✓	
Class note taker	87	✓	✓	✓
Class observer	70	✓	✓	
Cloze	156	✓	✓	
Collaborative listening/viewing guide	100	✓	✓	✓
Collaborative strategic reading	79	✓	✓	
Community of learners	143	✓	✓	
Computer simulations	80	✓	✓	✓
Concept organization	39	✓	✓	
Concept wheel	66	✓		
Considering the source	98	✓	✓	
Cooperative listening	89	✓	✓	✓
Creating graphics	143	✓	✓	✓
Creative nonfiction writing: RAFT	125	✓	✓	✓
Defend your stance	135	✓	✓	
Differentiating between facts and opinions	88	✓	✓	
Directed expository reading	41	✓	✓	
Directed listening-thinking activity	90	✓	✓	✓
Directed reading-thinking activity	40	✓	✓	✓
Discussing emotions	70	✓	✓	
Discussing facts and opinions	74	✓	✓	
Discussion prompts	74	✓	✓	
Dissecting essay questions	134	✓	✓	

Content Area Correlation Chart *(cont.)*

Strategy Name	Page(s)	Social Studies	Science	Math
Distinguishing between fiction and nonfiction	16	✓	✓	
Editing conferences	122	✓	✓	
Educator observation checklists	171–172	✓	✓	✓
Enabling questions	87	✓	✓	
Envisioning text while reading	50	✓	✓	
Essay templates	134	✓	✓	
Essential questions	64	✓		
Examining the author's motivation	68	✓	✓	
Experience writing	123	✓		
Film discussion	86	✓	✓	
Finding the main idea & details	51	✓	✓	
Five fingers	102	✓	✓	
Focus frame	34	✓	✓	
Formulating leads and conclusions	121	✓	✓	
Free association	38	✓	✓	
GIST: Finding the main idea	51	✓	✓	
Guided imagery	152	✓	✓	
Guided reading procedure	132	✓	✓	
Herringbone	164	✓		
Hierarchy array	23	✓	✓	
Home-school folder	108	✓	✓	✓
Important word parts in English	29	✓	✓	
Independent mind maps	101	✓	✓	✓
Informal notes outline	112	✓	✓	
Inquiry chart	148	✓	✓	
Inquiry-based research	139	✓	✓	
Interactive reading guide	80	✓	✓	✓
Internalized response	102	✓	✓	
Introducing new vocabulary	28	✓	✓	
Jackdaws	152	✓	✓	
Jigsaw	78	✓	✓	✓
Judicious highlighting	103	✓	✓	
Key sentences	126	✓	✓	✓
Key word imaging	103	✓	✓	✓
Key word notes	114	✓	✓	✓
Knowing where to look for answers	144	✓	✓	✓
Knowledge rating	22	✓	✓	✓
Knowledge tier	118	✓	✓	✓
K-W-L chart	150	✓	✓	✓
Learning logs	120	✓	✓	✓
Letters to the editor	135	✓	✓	
Levels of comprehension guide	91	✓	✓	

Content Area Correlation Chart *(cont.)*

Strategy Name	Page(s)	Social Studies	Science	Math
Life experiences vocabulary	103	✓		
Listening guide	90	✓	✓	✓
Listening to different points of view	86	✓	✓	
Listen-read-discuss	87	✓	✓	✓
List-group-label	19	✓	✓	
Magnet summaries	128	✓	✓	✓
Main idea: Balancing bar	94	✓	✓	
Main idea: Equation	160	✓	✓	✓
Main idea: Greek temple	54	✓	✓	
Main idea: Pyramid	52	✓	✓	
Opinion and support diamond	136	✓	✓	
Paraphrasing a song	129	✓		
Peer editing	122	✓	✓	
Performances	154	✓	✓	✓
Portfolios	155	✓	✓	✓
Possible sentences	90	✓	✓	
Praise-question-polish	122	✓	✓	
Question exchange	105	✓	✓	✓
Question-answer relationships	48	✓	✓	
Questioning the author	72	✓	✓	
Questions on trial	45	✓	✓	
Quick review	101	✓	✓	✓
Quick writes	18	✓	✓	✓
Reaction guide	89	✓	✓	
Read alouds	16	✓	✓	
Readers guild	79	✓		
Recognizing persuasive language	88	✓		
ReQuest	44	✓	✓	
Rethinking traditional test items	158	✓	✓	✓
Roundtable alphabet	116	✓	✓	✓
Roundtable discussions	77	✓		
Scattergories	106	✓		
Schema activation plan	24	✓	✓	
Scoring guides	166–170	✓	✓	✓
Seeing it from both sides	71	✓	✓	
Selective reading guide	41	✓	✓	
Self-monitoring reading strategy	42	✓	✓	✓
Semantic matrix	20	✓	✓	
Signal words	56	✓	✓	
Songs and rhymes	101	✓	✓	✓
SQ3R	104	✓	✓	✓
Stairstep sequencer	58	✓		

Content Area Correlation Chart *(cont.)*

Strategy Name	Page(s)	Social Studies	Science	Math
Strategic questioning	37	✓	✓	
Student achievement teams	77	✓	✓	✓
Student self-evaluation forms	173	✓	✓	✓
Sum it up chart	146	✓		
Summarizing	104	✓	✓	✓
Summary frame	130	✓	✓	✓
Summary grid	81	✓		
Surveys	142	✓	✓	✓
Sustained summary writing	129	✓	✓	
Taking a stand	71	✓	✓	
Teaching inferential skills	56	✓	✓	
Text-response centers	115	✓	✓	
Text structure	57	✓	✓	
Think alouds	36	✓		
Thinking guide	32	✓	✓	
Timelines	60	✓	✓	
Turning headings into questions	45	✓	✓	✓
Understanding and using textbook parts	17	✓	✓	✓
Unlock the meanings of new words	28	✓	✓	
Using a computer for research	145	✓	✓	
Using active verbs	121	✓	✓	
Using the library for research	145	✓	✓	
Venn diagram (2-circle)	61	✓	✓	
Venn diagram (3-circle)	62	✓	✓	
Visual syntetics	71	✓	✓	✓
Visualizing while listening	84	✓	✓	
Vocabulary into essay	162	✓	✓	✓
Voice	86	✓	✓	
Weighing the choices	96	✓	✓	
What are the features of nonfiction works?	80	✓	✓	
What I want to know is…	46	✓	✓	
Why? Pie	82	✓	✓	
Word association	17	✓	✓	
Word trees	30	✓	✓	
Writing about a past event	123	✓		
Writing in response to text	124	✓	✓	✓
Written reports	153	✓	✓	
You are there	102	✓		
You're in the picture	24	✓		

Introduction to Section 1: Preparing Students for Nonfiction

Successfully teaching nonfiction means "arousing the curiosity of students, assessing their present understandings, exploring with them some of the possibilities for study about the topic, and . . . setting the stage for learning to take place" (Parker, 2001). This section gives you techniques for getting students to think about what they already know so that they will take in new information and incorporate it into their store of knowledge. The larger a person's store of information, the more apt he or she is to successfully comprehend and learn new material.

Nonfiction text is packed with both concepts and vocabulary. Before students can truly comprehend nonfiction material, you must always activate their background knowledge (schema). If your students are unfamiliar with a topic you are about to study, it is even more crucial for you to spend time building their knowledge foundation.

Competent readers and listeners interact with information, consciously thinking of questions, revising predictions, and eliminating misconceptions. For information to enter long-term memory, students must not only integrate new data with their previous store of knowledge, they must also to be able to transfer this new knowledge to different or new situations. In addition, authors expect readers to use their own experiences and knowledge to interact with information. Therefore, your students must learn the inferential skills necessary to "read between the lines" and understand implied ideas that are not stated. For methods of developing students' inferential skills, see the Reading Nonfiction section.

Strategies: Read Alouds; Distinguishing Between . . .

❖ Read Alouds

One of the best ways to prepare students for expository text is to read nonfiction aloud to them daily. Reading expository text aloud is critical to developing your students' ability to read it. This is true even in high school. Discussion can never replace reading aloud because people rarely speak using the vocabulary and complex sentence structures of written language.

Making predictions is a good way to make students tap into their prior knowledge, so read the beginning of a passage, then stop and ask them to predict what might occur. Do this at several points throughout your reading of the text. Over time you will find that your students' ability to make accurate predictions will increase tremendously.

❖ Distinguishing Between Fiction and Nonfiction

Help your students think about the differences between fiction and nonfiction by reading aloud a story (such as an Aesop's fable) and a nonfiction article (*Time for Kids* magazine). Guide a class discussion with these questions:

- How are stories (fiction) and nonfiction articles the same?
- How are stories and nonfiction articles different?
- Why are stories and nonfiction articles different?
- Should we read nonfiction articles the same way that we read stories? Explain.

Strategies: Parts of a Textbook; Pictures; Word Association

✜ Understanding and Using the Parts of a Textbook

An enjoyable way to teach students about the parts of a textbook is to have small groups read together and fill out a form to discover the purpose of textbook formatting. Suppose you have groups preview chapter 18, which is about oceans and the water cycle. Ask them to identify at least four kinds of text that is formatted differently and record it on the chart:

Page Number	Text	How It Stands Out	What's the Purpose?
173	water cycle	bold print	side heading (for new section)
173	evaporation	italics	vocabulary word
174	Note	footnote at bottom	tells where idea came from (source)
179	Jacques Cousteau	red print	key person

✜ A Picture Is Worth a Thousand Words

Show a documentary or fictional film prior to teaching about an event. For example, before studying the attack on Pearl Harbor, have your students watch a film such as *Pearl Harbor* or *Tora, Tora, Tora*. Be sure to view the film first to be certain that it is appropriate for your grade level. Depending on your district's policy, you may also need written parental permission before showing a fictional film.

✜ Word Association

Bolster your students' vocabulary by displaying three or four words from an upcoming passage or topic. Challenge your students to come up with words that relate to each (not necessarily synonyms) and add them to the list. For example, you display these boldface words:

transport	**precipice**	**expressway**
move	cliff	traffic
carry	steep	vehicles
airplane	rocks	highway
truck	crag	road
train	bluff	exit

Strategies: Quick Writes; Analogies; Categorizing

❖ Quick Writes

Quick writes (Moore, et al., 1998) are an excellent way of preparing students to assimilate new material by having them mentally retrieve and write previously learned material. For example, if you are going to read a passage about biomes, make certain that students know what the word means. Then state: "In the next minute I want you to write the name of every different kind of biome you know and any words that are related to each of the biomes." A student list might look like this:

desert—hot, dry, sand, thirsty

rain forest—hot, dark, huge trees, rare plants

tundra—cold, windy, almost no plants, polar bears

This technique will let students approach the biomes chapter with greater confidence: it makes them realize that they already know something about the topic. The realization that they already possess some knowledge empowers struggling students.

❖ Analogy as an Introduction

To make expository text more comprehensible, use activities that tap into students' feelings and experiences through the use of analogies. Prepare a short paragraph that highlights an analogy to which the students can relate. Have them read the analogy paragraph silently and then discuss it. For example, at the start of a unit on the Revolutionary War, you could present this analogy:

Have you ever fought with a friend? Did you hit or shout at your friend? How did your friend react? Did he or she shout back or hit you? Did your fight last so long that you wondered if you would ever be friends again? During the Revolutionary War, the American colonies faced a similar problem. Some colonists wanted to stay British citizens. Others wanted to form a new nation. This led to the Revolutionary War, with the colonists fighting against Britain. No one knew if Britain and the United States would ever be friends again.

❖ Categorizing

Categorization activities help students make inferences about clusters of related words. In the example, the students have been instructed to put each word under the part of a solar system that is most apt to have the characteristic. Each word can only go in one of the columns.

hot gas	rarely seen	rock	orbit
heat	frozen	light	supernova
tail	ice	atmosphere	sun

planets	stars	comets
rock	hot gas	rarely seen
orbit	light	ice
atmosphere	supernova	frozen
sun	heat	tail

The chart can spark discussion about where items belong—for example, comets orbit the sun, too, although with much less frequency than any of the planets. You can expand the chart throughout the unit by adding columns and characteristics of moons, asteroids, meteorites, etc.

Strategies: List-Group-Label

✣ List-Group-Label

You can use a list-group-label activity (Tierney, Readence, & Dishner, 1990) to help your students develop stronger conceptual and text-processing abilities. Give the students a topic. As a class, brainstorm for two minutes anything that relates to the concept. Do not judge or correct any suggestion; record them all. Post the list and put the students into teams of three. Each team's goal is to find three words on the list that form some type of group and provide a label for them. They should create as many groups as possible in five minutes. Make sure that your students understand the following rules:

- The commonality cannot be "words that end in e," "words that start with m," or "words that have a long vowel sound," etc.
- Terms can be used more than once.
- Some terms may not fit into any category.
- The label does not need to come from the list.

Example: Brainstorm every word you can think of related to plants:

beans	daffodils	wood	grass	roots	bushes
pine tree	leaves	dandelions	fruits	wheat	yard
evergreen	tulips	stem	roses	dirt	bark
pine cones	peas	corn	farm	vegetables	cactus
cherries	pineapples	daisies	raspberries	sunshine	food
mushrooms	strawberries	water	medicine	forest	green

Possible groups and labels (in bold print):

bushes—raspberries, roses, evergreen

vegetables—corn, peas, beans

farm crops—wheat, corn, beans

flowers—roses, daisies, daffodils

plant needs—water, dirt, sunshine

garden—strawberries, corn, green

tree parts—wood, bark, leaves

things we get from plants—wood, medicine, food

plant parts—leaves, roots, stem

fruits—cherries, pineapples, raspberries

evergreen—pine tree, pine cones, bark

in a yard—dirt, grass, dandelions

Discuss the students' groups and labels, gently correcting any that are wrong. After discussing the students' groupings, note any items that did not fit in any category. In this example, we did not place mushrooms in any category. This is a teachable moment—the ideal opportunity to explain why mushrooms are not plants: scientists classify them as a part of the fungi phylum because they cannot do photosynthesis or make their own food but must absorb it.

Strategies: Semantic Matrix

✤ Semantic Matrix

After students have had experience with list-group-label categorization, you can introduce a semantic matrix (Johnson & Pearson, 1984). This technique works best with concrete, familiar categories. The matrix helps students establish generalizations. Generalizations enable them to:

- remember properties and connect them to related items (a person who knows a turtle relates it to a new creature—such as a tortoise)

- recognize new examples (the person notices that a tortoise resembles a turtle)

- predict attributes of new examples (the person knows that turtles lay eggs and assumes that tortoises do, too)

Some of the words in the matrix must be familiar to the students so that they have a frame of reference. Fill in as much of the chart as you can prior to reading. If you know that the article will cover the information, do not tell the class if they agree to fill in a slot incorrectly. For this example, you are going to be teaching about water animals. You believe that many of your students are not familiar with barracuda or haddock but are familiar with dolphins and sharks. On a blank copy of page 21, set up your chart using both the new concepts and related words that are everyday concepts for your students. Distribute copies to the class and fill in the chart using these symbols:

+ (Yes)   – (No)   ? (Don't Know)

	carnivore	omnivore	lives in salt water	fish	live birth	dangerous to humans
barracuda	+	?	+	+	–	+
haddock	?	?	+	+	–	–
bass	?	?	–	+	–	–
shark	+	–	+	?	+	+
dolphin	?	?	+	?	+	–

The question marks set the purpose for reading. As you read the passage, stop whenever you encounter information that enables you to eliminate the question marks or to correct misconceptions. Question marks that remain after reading give you a chance to address how to look for answers. (Consult a resource such as the Internet, an encyclopedia, almanac, or atlas, etc.)

Semantic matrixes help students to evaluate and differentiate between things. For example, they may never have thought about the fact that water animals must live in either fresh or salt water and that putting them in the wrong kind of water will injure or even kill them. Even many adults don't realize that sharks are fish, not mammals. They get confused because sharks give birth to live young. You can make such observations while discussing the chart.

Strategies: Semantic Matrix *(cont.)*

Graphic Organizer

Directions: Fill out the chart using the following symbols:

+ (for **Yes**)   – (for **No**)   ? (for **Don't Know**)

Strategies: Knowledge Rating

✛ Knowledge Rating

A simple way for students to share with you what they already know about the specialized vocabulary of a topic is a knowledge rating sheet (Blachowicz & Ogle, 2001). Choose five vocabulary words that are crucial to understanding an upcoming expository passage. Using the graphic organizer at the bottom of this page, write the vocabulary words. Make photocopies and distribute. Read the words aloud to ensure that decoding is not an issue. Depending upon the needs of your class, give the students between 45 and 60 seconds to fill in the sheet and submit it to you. The following is an example:

Topic: Fractions

Directions: Put a checkmark (✓) in the column that tells how well you know each of these words.

Word	I know what it means.	I've heard it before.	I don't know it.
numerator	✓		
denominator	✓		
mixed number		✓	
reciprocal			✓
common factor			✓

- -

Graphic Organizer

Name: _____

Topic:

Directions: Put a checkmark (✓) in the column that tells how well you know each of these words.

Word	I know what it means.	I've heard it before.	I don't know it.

Strategies: Hierarchy Array

✥ Hierarchy Array

A hierarchy array depicts superior and subordinate relationships. Use one prior to studying something that has classifications and categories. For example:

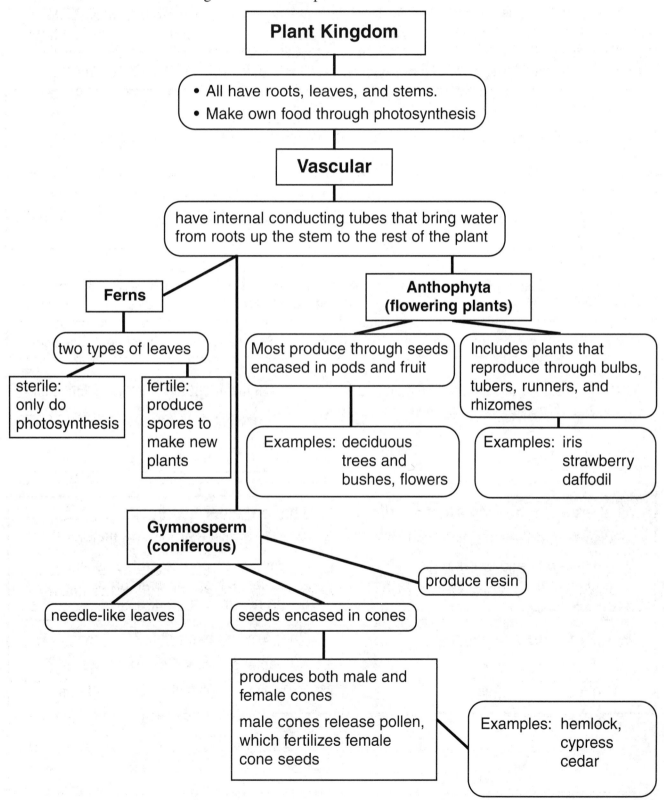

Strategies: You're in the Picture; Schema Activation Plan

✢ You're in the Picture

Science and social studies textbooks are loaded with illustrations and graphics to help students to understand new, unfamiliar concepts. To ensure that your students can begin visualizing the moment they begin reading text, always have them preview a chapter. Add a visualization element by stopping at a photo and having students concentrate on it. Say, "Don't look away from the photo. You have now entered the photo. You are actually there. What do you see? smell? hear? taste? What do you feel (emotion)? Now you are coming out of the photo. Let's discuss our experiences."

✢ Schema Activation Plan

To activate background knowledge, use a schema activation plan (Frayer, et al., 1969) prior to reading a nonfiction passage.

1. Preview the material; select a key concept; and then choose a phrase, picture, or word to represent it to your class to initiate a discussion.

2. Ask students to brainstorm everything they know about the topic. Create a master list on the board or overhead. Brainstorming is very important, since listening to the associations and explanations of others causes students to add to their own knowledge and helps you to determine the level of prior knowledge that your students have about the subject. This also empowers academically weak students by letting them know that they already have some knowledge about the topic to be studied.

3. Have the students summarize what they've learned through the use of the graphic organizer on page 25. Here's an example of a completed one:

What Are Fungi?

What are the most important features?	What are other features?		
• dissolve and absorb their food • can live on dead or living plants and animals	• cannot move around on their own • can cause people problems like athlete's foot and oral thrush (trench mouth), etc.		
What are some examples?	**What are *not* examples?**		
mushrooms mildew mold yeast	bacteria virus warts moss animals plants		

Strategies: Schema Activation Plan *(cont.)*

Graphic Organizer

What are _____ ?

What are the most important features?	What are other features?
What are some examples?	**What are *not* examples?**

Strategies: Anticipation Guide

⁘ Anticipation Guide

Use an anticipation guide to assess prior knowledge and to determine if your students have misconceptions about a topic. Using the graphic organizer on page 27, create an anticipation guide with a total of four or five true and false statements. Photocopy and distribute the guide. Read the statements to the students to avoid decoding issues. Then ask the students to mark each statement true or false.

After reading or listening to the information, have students fix any statements they marked incorrectly by writing a brief explanation of the correct answer. For example:

Lightning

Directions: Before you learn about thunderstorms, read these sentences. Based on what you already know about the topic, write **T** on the line if the statement is true and **F** on the line if the statement is false.

____F____ 1. Lightning cannot strike the same place twice.

Lightning can hit the same place many times. The Empire State Building is struck about two dozen times every single year.

____T____ 2. A direct hit by lightning can set a tree on fire.

____F____ 3. Lightning is bad for Earth's atmosphere.

Lightning produces ozone, which helps our atmosphere. It also reduces air pollutants by forcing them to fall to the ground.

____F____ 4. You will always hear a thunderclap before a lightning flash.

You hear the thunderclap after the lightning flash.

____T____ 5. Ball lightning is the rarest form of lightning.

Strategies: Anticipation Guide *(cont.)*

Graphic Organizer

Directions: Before you read about _____ ,
look at these sentences. Based on what you already know about the topic, write **T** on the line if
the statement is true and **F** on the line if the statement is false.

_____ 1.

_____ 2.

_____ 3.

_____ 4.

_____ 5.

Strategies: Vocabulary;
Unlock the Meaning

✣ Introducing New Vocabulary

Select a main concept with which the students will be familiar from an article to be read. Display the word and give the students three minutes in which to write as many related words as possible. Record a master list of student ideas underneath the concept word. Then add new, unfamiliar vocabulary words and discuss them.

Suppose you are about to read about the storm of the century, which occurred in March 1993 when a nor'easter blowing southwest from the Arctic Circle collided with a moisture-laden Gulf Stream, resulting in intense storms all along the eastern seaboard and an immense blizzard in the Northeast. Choose the basic concept of snow and have the students list their ideas.

snowman	snowplow	gloves	boots	storm
winter	snowboard	sledding	skiing	icicles
flakes	frost	slush	mittens	hats
cold	ice	shovel	scarves	whiteout
snowsuit	December	January	February	Christmas
blizzard	*frostbite*	*nor' easter*	*Arctic Circle*	*Gulf Stream*

The students come up with everything they already know about snow. Now you add the concepts (italicized) you want to discuss. Since the students are already in a "snowy" state of mind, their minds will more readily incorporate these new concepts.

✣ Unlock the Meanings of New Words

Affixes are prefixes or suffixes added to a root word. Students need to recognize common word parts to unlock the meanings of new words. Introduce the concept of affixes by giving examples of a few from the chart on page 29 and asking students to suggest any they know. In this way you will find out which ones the students already know, and you will not need to spend any time studying those.

Teach students to cover affixes as soon as they recognize them so that they can concentrate on the root. Next they should uncover the prefix, then the suffix, and finally put the word together.

Be alert to opportunities of pointing out words from many sources (on the Internet, in fiction reading, or during a video or television show) that have affixes and roots. Guide students to determine what they mean using what they already know.

When teaching prefixes and suffixes, it is wise to give the students a group of words that they already know, such as *unable, unhappy, unimportant, unwise, undo,* and *unkind.* Ask them to identify the common letters (*un*). Explain that this is a prefix used with many words. Have the class think about what the words mean. Ask for volunteers to give you definitions. Write these on the board. Ask the students if they can detect what the word part means.

Strategies: Word Parts

✛ **Important Word Parts in English**

Suffix	Meaning	Prefix	Meaning	Root	Meaning
-s or -es	plural	un-	not	act	do
-ed	verb ending	re-	again	ast	star
-ing	verb ending	in-, im-	not	cycl	circle
-ly	like, every	dis-	opposite	fac	make, do
-er, -or	one who	en-, em-	in	form	shape
-ition, -ation	state or quality of	non-	not	gram	letter, written
-able, -ible	inclined to, apt to	over-	too much	graph	write
-al, -ial	relating to	mis-	bad	man	hand
-ness	state or quality of	sub-	below	meter	measure
-ity, -ty	state or quality of	pre-	before	bio	life
-ment	action or product	inter-	among, between	geo	earth
-ic	system	fore-	before, in front	ped	foot
-ous, -ious	state or quality of	de-	opposite	phon	sound
-en	relating to	trans-	across	photo	light
-tive, -sive, -ive	inclined to, apt to	super-	over, more than	port	carry
-ful	full of	semi-	partial, half	scope	see
-less	without	anti-	against	spect	see
-er	more (comparative)	mid-	middle	struct	build, form
-est	most (superlative)	under-	too little, below	therm	heat

Prefixes and suffixes are from White, T., et al. (1989) "Teaching Elementary Students to Use Word-Part Clues." *The Reading Teacher*, 42, 302–309.

Roots were selected from Fry, E., et al. (2000) *The Reading Teacher's Book of Lists.* Center for Applied Research in Education.

Strategies: Word Trees

⁜ Word Trees

Just as trees grow from roots, many words also "grow" from roots. One way to teach roots is to create and display word trees. Give students an opportunity to guess at what the root "graph" means (to write in a way that can be seen). Explain that even if the students don't know the meaning of all the words in the tree, they now know that each word must have something to do with writing that can be seen.

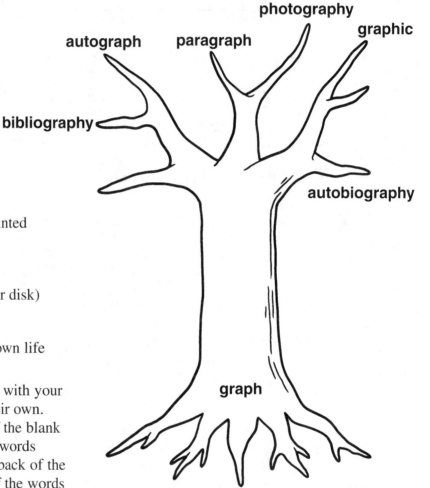

- ✧ **bibliography:**
  a list of materials used
  to write a report

- ✧ **autograph:**
  a person's signature

- ✧ **paragraph:**
  a group of three or more
  sentences about the same topic

- ✧ **graphic:**
  something written, drawn, or printed

- ✧ **photography:**
  making pictures with a camera
  (pictures are "written" on film or disk)

- ✧ **autobiography:**
  an account written about one's own life

Directions: Do several of these trees with your class; then have them try a few on their own. For example, you can make a copy of the blank tree on page 31 and write the "form" words listed below in the branches. On the back of the paper write sentences that use each of the words in the branches. Photocopy (double-sided) and distribute. Pair the students and ask them to identify the common root (set of letters). Then, after reading the sentences on the back, see if they can define what the root (form) must mean. Ask them to write a definition for the words in the branches. "Form" means "to give shape," as is illustrated by these examples:

- ✧ conform = to shape the same
- ✧ uniform = of the same shape as others
- ✧ reform = shape again to make it better

- ✧ format = to give a shape
- ✧ transform = change shape
- ✧ deform = ruin the shape

Strategies: Word Trees (cont.)

Graphic Organizer

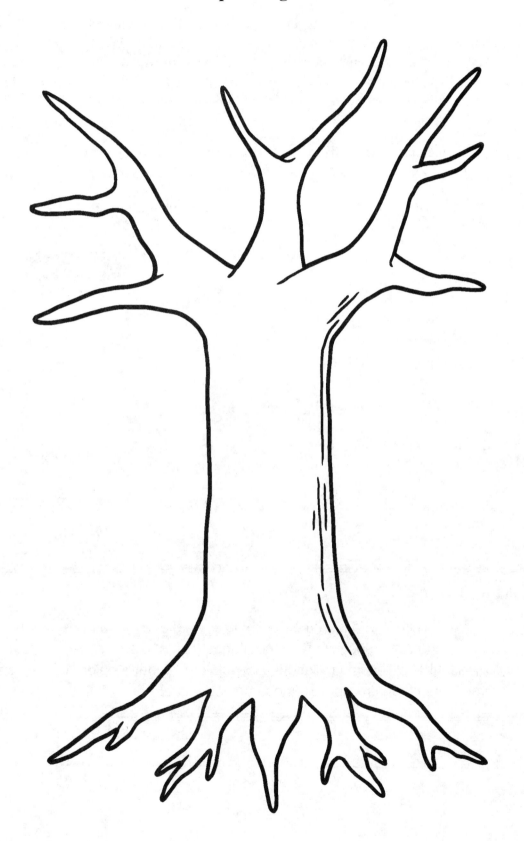

Strategies: Thinking Guide

⁜ Thinking Guide

Thinking guides (Herber, 1978) give your students a preview of the important concepts or issues that will be raised in an article. It also gets them to compare what they think about issues to what the author thinks. Fill in the thinking guide graphic organizer on page 33 with five statements. Photocopy and distribute the guide. Read the statements to the students to avoid decoding issues. In the **Me** column, the student writes an "A" for "agree" if he or she believes the statement is true or a "D" for "disagree" if he or she believes the statement is wrong.

After reading the passage, the student fills in the **Author** column. Then the student writes a paragraph about what was learned. The following is an example.

Directions: Read each statement. Write an **A** if you agree or a **D** if you disagree. You will fill in the author information and "What did you learn?" after reading.

	Me	Author
1. There isn't much we can do to stop disease.	D	D
2. Everyone in the world faces the same danger from disease	A	D
3. Today's diseases are much worse than those in the past.	A	D
4. A deadly disease is called an epidemic.	A	D
5. Vaccines can prevent the spread of disease.	A	A

What did you learn?

People who live in Third World countries, who have weakened immune systems, or who engage in unhealthy behaviors face the highest risk of disease. An epidemic is a deadly disease that spreads throughout a population. Today's epidemics—even AIDS—are no worse than smallpox or the bubonic plague.

Strategies: Thinking Guide *(cont.)*

Graphic Organizer

Directions: Read each statement. Write an **A** if you agree or a **D** if you disagree. You will fill in the author information and "What did you learn?" after you are finished reading.

	Me	Author
1.	_____	_____
2.	_____	_____
3.	_____	_____
4.	_____	_____
5.	_____	_____

What did you learn?

Strategies: Focus Frame

✛ Focus Frame

A focus frame offers an excellent way to tackle any expository reading assignment. To activate prior knowledge students preview the text, looking for vocabulary words they already know. Then they read the summary (or ending paragraphs) to see what's highlighted in the "wrap-up." Finally, they generate questions. This can be done as a whole class, with partners, or individually. To help students generate better questions, have them rank order their questions, with 1 being the most and 4 being the least. You can have the rank order based on the following:

♦ *importance* (most important to least important for understanding the subject);

♦ *prediction* (most apt to be answered by the reading to least apt);

♦ or *personal interest* (most interested in finding out to least interested in finding out, as in the example below).

When the students find the answers, they record them.

Focus Frame for
Iroquois Native Americans

1. Skim material for words that you already know. Write them.

   Iroquois   medicine man   venison

2. Read the chapter/article summary. What does it emphasize? Write at least two things.

   Iroquois created a League of Nations, where five tribes joined together in a loose government. The first New York State settlers probably wouldn't have survived without their help.

3. List four questions you have. Then rank them in order of:

   likely to be in the text   important for understanding the topic   personal interest

   One is the most and four is the least.

Rank	Questions
1	Q: What happened to them when they got sick? A: They had a medicine man who performed special rites and chants and used herbal cures.
3	Q: What were their homes like? A: Multiple families, all related through the mother, lived in bark-covered longhouses. There were bunks along the walls and smoke holes in the roof.
4	Q: What did they eat? A: They mostly ate venison, fish, turkeys, pheasants, and other wild animals that they caught using arrows. They grew corn, beans, squash, and berries.
2	Q: Did they have a method for reading and writing? A: Not answered by the chapter.

4. Write the answers to your questions as you find them in the text.

Strategies: Focus Frame *(cont.)*

Focus Frame for

_____

1. Skim material for words that you already know. Write them.

   _____

   _____

   _____

2. Read the chapter/article summary. What does it emphasize? Write at least two things.

   _____

   _____

   _____

3. List four questions you have. Then rank them in order of:

   likely to be in the text   **important for understanding the topic**   **personal interest**

   One is the most and four is the least.

Rank	Questions
	Q: A:
	Q: A:
	Q: A:
	Q: A:

4. Write the answers to your questions as you find them in the text.

Strategies: Think-Alouds; Organizer

✛ Think-Alouds

Modeling your own thought processes will develop your students' ability to make predictions and monitor their own comprehension. Model the reading of an expository text by briefly previewing the title, illustrations, and side headings. Ask the students to predict what the passage might be about. Read aloud to a good stopping point. Ask a question about what has happened so far in the text. Do a "think aloud"—that is, share your metacognitive processes by summarizing what's been read so far and making a prediction such as "I think _____ will happen next." Ask the students if they agree with your prediction. If they don't, have them state their own predictions. Remember to occasionally give a wrong prediction: if yours are always right, the students will realize that and never suggest their own. Read aloud to the next good stopping point in the passage. This time ask the students a question, "What do you think the author means when she says . . .? What makes you think so? Can you give an example?" Ask the students what they believe will happen next. Read to the end of the passage. Discuss the selection as a whole, being certain to talk about the predictions that were made and how things would have been changed if the incorrect predictions had come true.

✛ Advanced Organizer

When you anticipate that the text will be especially challenging, give an advanced organizer (Ausubel, 1978) to help students focus on the important details. Have the students read the advanced organizer before reading or listening to a passage. This sets a purpose and promotes careful, active reading or listening. Then, after the students have read or heard the information, they fill in the advanced organizer. An example appears below.

Scientists keep track of the Earth's _____. They found a problem in

the _____ layer. There was too little _____ .

They discovered that _____ were causing the trouble. CFCs were put

into _____ , _____ , and _____.

The scientists made people understand the problem. So, by the mid 1990s, CFCs were

no longer _____ .

The actual passage would read something like this:

Scientists have kept track of the Earth's atmosphere for a long time. During the mid 1970s they found a problem: the top layer of air was getting too thin. There was not enough ozone. Scientists wanted to know why. They found out that CFCs from spray cans, refrigerators, and air conditioners were the cause. The scientists told the world about the problem. Finally, by the mid 1990s companies had stopped putting CFCs in their products.

Strategies: Strategic Questioning

✛ Strategic Questioning

Strategic Questioning (King, 1991) is a good way to help students overcome a lack of prior knowledge about a topic. It enables students to build new knowledge by listening to each other.

1. Start by telling the students the title of the passage and asking this set of questions:

   ◆ What kind of information do you expect to read?

   ◆ What kind of illustrations do you expect to see?

   ◆ Do you have any knowledge about this topic? Please share it.

2. Preview the text by doing the following:

   ◆ reading the title, side headings, and italicized or bold print words

   ◆ scanning any fine print questions in the margins (usually found only in textbooks)

   ◆ skimming any pictures, diagrams, charts, time lines, or graphs

3. Next, ask some of these questions (whichever ones seem most appropriate for the specific passage):

   ◆ Have you read any other works by this author? What do you think of them?

   ◆ How can we change the side headings into questions?

   ◆ Which words are emphasized (appear in bold or italic print)?

   ◆ Why do you think the author chose to emphasize those words?

   ◆ What do you think the main idea will be?

   ◆ What graphics (pictures, graphs, charts, time lines, and diagrams) are included?

   ◆ How do we read these graphics?

   ◆ Why do you think these particular graphics were included?

Strategic questioning may reveal that your students lack sufficient background knowledge to handle the topic. If this occurs, use additional strategies from this section.

Strategies: Free Association

✛ Free Association

Activate background knowledge through free association. Present the two major concepts of expository text and ask students to generate a list of ideas relating to each. Challenge them to find a way in which the ideas in the lists relate to each other.

Suppose you plan to read an article about how the suburbs are sprawling dangerously close to Mount Washington, an active (though dormant) volcano. The article discusses pending legislation that will prohibit building any closer. You plan to have a class discussion on whether or not people have a legal right to continue to build housing developments so close to a volcano.

Directions: Divide the class in half. The students in one half of the class will have two minutes to individually brainstorm a list of words relating to volcanoes. At the same time the students in the other half of the class will individually brainstorm a list of words relating to suburbs.

Volcanoes		Suburbs	
• hot	• dangerous	•streets	• trees
• lava	• smoke	•parks	• people
• Hawaii	• ash	•stores	• schools
• scary	• mountain	•library	• offices
• fire	• poison gas (sulfur)	•houses	• fire department

Generate a class list to which the students can refer. Then put the students into teams of three. Each team should try to generate pairs of words (using one from each list). They must be able to orally defend their pairings. Words can be paired more than once. Here's an example of a student list:

> **dangerous** and **streets**—"It's dangerous to run into the street without looking."
>
> **dangerous** and **fire department**—"Fire departments respond to dangerous situations."
>
> **smoke** and **houses**—"When a volcano or a house burns, there is lots of smoke."
> "Smoke comes out of the top of a volcano and out of houses' chimneys."
>
> **Hawaii** and **parks**—"Hawaii has active volcanoes and beautiful parks."
>
> **fire** and **fire department**—"The fire department responds to a fire."

From the associations students made, they may anticipate that one of the issues presented in the article is that building homes close to a volcano poses undue jeopardy and hardship on local firefighters and fire departments in the event of an eruption.

Strategies: Concept Organization

✛ Concept Organization

Concept organization charts ensure all students have a frame of reference prior to tackling expository information. Suppose you are going to read a passage about a power station in France that generates electricity through the rise and fall of the tides. With this graphic organizer, you give a broad category—in this instance, ways to generate electricity. Draw on the board or overhead the simple graphic shown below. List ways that electricity can be generated. Then, guide the students to come up with the advantages and disadvantages of each method of creating electrical power, listing them beneath each type. This will activate the students' schema about electrical power as well as provide a valuable overview for students who know little or nothing about the subject.

Ways to Generate Electricity

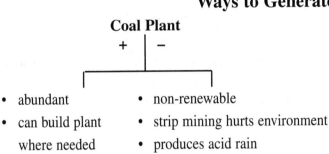

Coal Plant

+	−
• abundant	• non-renewable
• can build plant where needed	• strip mining hurts environment
• lower dependence on foreign oil	• produces acid rain
	• hard to transport
	• greenhouse gases/global warming

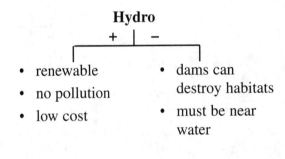

Natural Gas

+	−
• easy to transport	• diminishing supply
• relatively cheap	• greenhouse gases
• can build plant where needed	• non-renewable
• burns cleaner than coal	

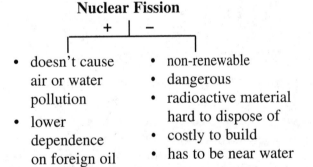

Nuclear Fission

+	−
• doesn't cause air or water pollution	• non-renewable
• lower dependence on foreign oil	• dangerous
	• radioactive material hard to dispose of
	• costly to build
	• has to be near water

Hydro

+	−
• renewable	• dams can destroy habitats
• no pollution	• must be near water
• low cost	

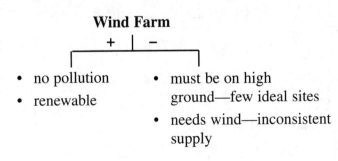

Wind Farm

+	−
• no pollution	• must be on high ground—few ideal sites
• renewable	• needs wind—inconsistent supply

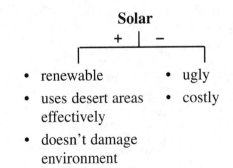

Solar

+	−
• renewable	• ugly
• uses desert areas effectively	• costly
• doesn't damage environment	

Introduction to Section 2: Reading Nonfiction

Reading is the foundation of learning, and nonfiction reading comprises the bulk of what students will see and use. Students must become strategic readers who approach expository text with confidence. However, the skills needed for reading nonfiction are not exactly the same as those used for reading fiction. This means that students need direct instruction, guided practice, and a lot of support and encouragement. Because reading is such a multifaceted activity requiring so many skills, the strategies in this section are grouped in the following order:

- **guiding reading**—beginning with DRTA on this page
- **self-monitoring while reading nonfiction**—on page 42
- **asking questions before, during, and after reading**—beginning on page 43
- **envisioning text while reading**—on page 50
- **finding the main idea and supporting details**—beginning on page 51
- **making inferences based on recognition of signal words**—on page 56
- **understanding text structure**—beginning on page 57
- **time order and sequencing**—on page 60
- **comparing/contrasting**—beginning on page 61
- **summarizing**—beginning on page 64
- **thinking about the author's motivation**—beginning on page 68

Strategies: DRTA

❖ DRTA

Use a Directed Reading and Thinking Activity (DRTA) (Stauffer, 1969) to prepare students to independently read expository text. Scaffold your instruction by working with the whole group, then move to small groups or partners, and finally to independent work. Divide the text to be read into meaningful segments—often two or three paragraphs. For each section, follow these steps:

1. **Preview**—When students preview text, we tell them to attend to the title and side headings, but they may not know what to do other than look at them. So teach them to turn the titles and side headings into questions by doing one of the following:
   - adding a question mark at the end (*example*: Cirrus clouds?)
   - putting "What is" or "What are" in front of the heading (*example*: What are cirrus clouds?)
   - turning the heading into a cloze statement (*example*: Cirrus clouds _____ .).

2. **Predict**—Have the students make one prediction and jot it in a learning log.

3. **Read**—They read to prove or disprove their prediction. The reading may be done silently or aloud, alone or with others.

4. **Prove**—After reading the selection, have the students write "True" or "False" next to their predictions. If their predictions are false, ask them to state what they could change to make them true.

Strategies: Expository Reading; Reading Guide

✦ Directed Expository Reading

Try the directed expository reading procedure with a lesson from which you would like the students to remember the most facts. Here are the steps:

1. Choose a technique to cover the vocabulary and to activate prior knowledge (from the Preparing Students for Nonfiction section).

2. Have the students read the passage to themselves silently.

3. Have the students set aside the text and, without referring to it, recall all the information that they can. Record on the board or overhead all the statements the students make (even those that are wrong) without commenting.

4. When no one can recall any more, send the students back to the text to reread and check the accuracy of the statements.

5. Have the students set the text aside again and correct any inaccuracies in the statements. At this point they can also add more information obtained from the second reading.

6. Pair the students and ask them to create a summary, outline, or graphic organizer that includes all the facts. Make photocopies of their work so that each of the partners has a copy.

7. After they have completed that task, ask, "How does this information relate to what we learned (last month, last week, yesterday)?"

8. The students individually study their summaries, outlines, or graphic organizers in preparation for a test.

✦ Selective Reading Guide

Prepare a Selective Reading Guide (Cunningham & Shablak, 1975) to teach students to use their textbooks as a resource rather than as a tome that must be read cover to cover. This is especially effective with struggling or reluctant readers because it notifies them about what information is the most essential. Here's an example:

---

page 186

Paragraphs 1 & 2—Introduce the section. Read them quickly.

Paragraphs 3 & 4—Define an ocean and its importance to our planet. Know the names of world's oceans and their locations on a world map or globe.

---

page 187

Paragraph 1—Based on the information in this paragraph, make a list of the world's five oceans in order of their size in your journal.

Paragraphs 2 & 3—Pay attention to the differences in the oceans' average temperatures and their effect on the world's weather.

Paragraphs 4 & 5—Skim these paragraphs.

Strategies: Self Monitoring

❖ Self-Monitoring Reading Strategy

Vaughen & Estes (1986) encourage readers to ask questions and independently find answers. Prominently display a poster stating the steps in this strategy. Direct the students to refer to the poster often. The strategy is best taught through several series of think-alouds in materials that you personally find challenging.

☞ **Step 1:** Do I understand?

Read a paragraph. Then ask, "Do I totally understand everything in this paragraph?"

Use a pencil to put a light X next to each paragraph you totally comprehend and a light question mark next to each paragraph that contains anything that you do not understand.

☞ **Step 2:** What have I just read?

At the end of each paragraph stop and summarize silently to yourself in your own words what you have read. You may look back at the text during this activity.

☞ **Step 3:** Does it make sense now?

Finish reading the passage. Return to each paragraph that has a penciled question mark next to it and reread. Does it make sense now? If so, great! If not, move to step 4.

☞ **Step 4:** Why am I having this trouble?

Pinpoint the problem. Is the difficulty unfamiliar words or concepts? Is the sentence structure too complex? Is it because I know so little background information about the topic? Emphasize to students the importance of figuring out their specific stumbling blocks before moving to step 5.

☞ **Step 5:** Where can I get help?

Try a variety of aids: glossary, appendix, dictionary, chapter summary, etc. If confusion remains after going through these five steps, ask a classmate or teacher for assistance.

As students become more comfortable with this strategy, make a rule that the students cannot ask for help from you unless they can do the following:

- identify the exact source of their confusion

- describe the steps they've already taken on their own to resolve the problem

---

Strategies: Asking Questions

✥ Asking Questions Before, During, and After Reading

Before reading aloud a passage from a high school textbook in a content area with which you are not familiar, tell your class the questions you have and record each one on a sticky note (Harvey & Goudvis, 2000). As you read, stop and ask each question that occurs to you, writing it on a sticky note. When the text answers one of your questions, press the sticky note in the book's margin and code it "A" for answered. When you encounter a passage that confuses you, say "Huh?" and then reread to clarify. If you still don't understand, record a question mark on a sticky note, press it into the book's margin, and read further. When you encounter material that clears up your confusion, move the sticky note with the question mark to the appropriate place in the book's margin and draw a star on it to show that your confusion is gone. If your question remains unanswered after you have completed the passage, write a question on the sticky note and press it onto a sheet of notebook paper. This is a "research question" that you can then pursue in a variety of ways: by checking an encyclopedia, calling a high school content area teacher, doing online research, etc. Be sure to tell your students of your plan for finding the answer(s), and then follow through.

After you have modeled this questioning process, tackle a text with the whole class, using the same sticky-note technique. Once the students appear to understand the strategy, distribute sticky notes and ask them to code their own nonfiction reading. Use the following sticky-note code:

A—for directly answered by the text

I—for inferred from the text

R—for needs to be researched

U—for unknown and may never be known

Categorizing questions helps students to summarize material and to recognize that not all questions can be answered. The ultimate goal of questioning after reading is to summarize what's been learned and to prompt further investigation into questions that have not been answered (see Researching Nonfiction section).

Strategies: ReQuest

✣ ReQuest

Use ReQuest, or reciprocal questioning (Manzo, 1969), with a text in which it is possible to predict what the passage is about after reading the first three paragraphs. Read the passage in advance and determine stopping points where you will ask questions. Read aloud the first part. Stop and let the students ask you a question. Read the next section, and then ask the class a question.

Your questions help students to focus on what's important in a text. When you ask a question, remember the significance of wait time. After you ask a student a question, silently count to five (or ten if you have a student who struggles to put thoughts into words) before giving additional prompts or redirecting the question to another student. Continue taking turns asking and answering questions for the first three or four paragraphs. Then have students make predictions about the remainder of the expository passage and read it on their own. In the following example, the italicized words are the text:

What do apples, tomatoes, peaches, plums, and kiwis have in common? Besides the obvious answer of their classification as fruits, they emit ethylene gas (C2H4).

Student A: "Is a tomato really a fruit?"

Teacher: *(To student A)* "Yes. So is a pumpkin. Any fleshy body that encloses seeds is classified as a fruit. The fleshy part will decay to nourish the seeds."

Teacher: *(To class)* "What do you think ethylene gas is?"

Student A: "A chemical that the fruits release as they decompose."

Student B: "Another form of methane gas."

Student C: "Ethyl means alcohol, so it's probably a form of alcohol."

Teacher: "Choose a prediction, and then I'll read on and we'll see if it's right."

Without ethylene gas fruits would not ripen. The colorless, odorless gas is necessary for the fruit to mature. That is why putting fruits into a paper bag will help them ripen quickly. The ethylene gas stays trapped inside the bag and acts upon the fruit.

Teacher: "Which prediction was the closest?"

Teacher: *(After brief discussion)* "What do you think the article will talk about next?"

Strategies: Turning Headings into Questions; Questions on Trial

✦ Turning Headings into Questions

Students need practice turning a question into a partial statement and then looking for that statement to find the question's answer. Whenever you hand out questions related to a passage, have the students practice turning the questions into statements like this:

Question	Turned into a Statement to Look for in Text
What happens at a water treatment plant?	At a water treatment plant . . .
Why do two halves make a whole?	Two halves make a whole because . . .
How did President Lincoln die?	President Lincoln died when . . .

✦ Questions on Trial

Use the Questions on Trial strategy once your students understand the importance of asking questions before, during, and after reading. Create a panel of four student judges who will analyze their classmates' questions. The panel must explain why they believe a question is "good" or "better" *based on the question's ability to enhance the knowledge of the questioner.* There are no "bad" questions; only good questions and better questions. Assign your weakest students to be judges on the panel only after they have seen it in action several times. Here are some examples:

Good question: When did Christopher Columbus discover America?

Panel's analysis: *This is a good question, but it's very narrow. All you will learn from it is a date.*

Better question: Why did Christopher Columbus set sail across the Atlantic Ocean?

Panel's analysis: *This is a better question. It will lead you to a major understanding.*

Good question: How was Christopher Columbus received by the natives he met?

Panel's analysis: *This is a good question, especially if you give an explanation rather than a one-word answer.*

Better question: What were the consequences of Christopher Columbus's discovery of America?

Panel's analysis: *This is a better question because it will help you to find out what happened in the long run.*

Strategies: What I Want to Know Is . . .

✤ What I Want to Know Is . . .

To promote active reading through questioning, ask your students to record the questions they have before, during, and after they read an expository text. Have your students independently preview and then read a nonfiction passage, filling out the graphic organizer from page 47 at the appropriate intervals. Here's an example:

Write one question you have *before* reading. Write two questions you have *as you read*. Write one question you have *after you are finished* reading. Write the answers as you find them *in your own words*.

Before **page 196**	**Q:** What causes global warming? **A:** Global warming comes from carbon dioxide. The carbon dioxide is released from engines (cars, boats, etc.), factories, and homes all over the world.
While **page 197**	**Q:** Why is global warming bad for Earth? **A:** Global warming is bad for plants and animals. It changes the temperature of their natural environment. Food sources may die, and then plants and animals will have nothing to eat. If they cannot adapt, they will die.
While **page 199**	**Q:** What is being done to stop global warming? **A:** People are trying to pass laws to make cars and factories dump less carbon dioxide into the air. This will make the air cleaner and help stop global warming.
After	**Q:** Do world leaders have a plan for stopping global warming?

How can you find the answer?

I can ask my teacher, call a local meteorologist, read a book about global warming, check an encyclopedia, or research it on the Internet.

Strategies: What I Want to Know Is ... *(cont.)*

Graphic Organizer

Write one question you have before reading. Write two questions you have as you read. Write one question you have after you are finished reading. Write the answers as you find them in your own

Before   **Q:**

page _____   **A:**

While   **Q:**

page _____   **A:**

While   **Q:**

page _____   **A:**

After   **Q:**

How can you find the answer?

Strategies: Question-Answer Relationships

✥ Question-Answer Relationships

T. E. Raphael created the Question-Answer Relationships strategy (1982) to make students aware of the kinds of questions typically asked by textbooks, teachers, and tests. After the students have read a passage, provide a series of questions on the Question-Answer Relationships graphic organizer on page 49. Explain to the students that there are three kinds of answers:

1. **Stated (S)**—The answer is easy to find because the words used in the questions and the words in the text are identical. (See question #2 in the example below.)

2. **Look For It (L)**—The words used in the passage and the words in the question are different but similar. (See question #1 in the example below.)

3. **Think About It (T)**—The answer is not in the passage, and thus requires students to combine the text information with what they know to frame a response. (See question #3 in the example below.)

The students complete the graphic organizer by coding the questions and writing the answers in complete sentences in the spaces provided. The example is based on the following paragraph:

> Things like grass, garden clippings, and leaves make good compost. So do food scraps. You can make compost in a big box or a pile. You put organic (natural) waste material in and cover it with a layer of dirt to make the waste decay faster. After all of the material breaks down, it looks just like soil. Then you can put it on your garden. Mixing compost into soil gives it more nutrients and helps plants grow.

Code each question with one of these letters:

S = if the answer was stated

L = if you had to look for the answer

T = if you thought about it to come up with an answer; it wasn't in the text

Question	Code	Answer
1. What happens if you mix compost with dirt?	L	It makes the compost rot faster and makes the soil better for plants.
2. What things make good compost?	S	Grass, garden clippings, leaves, and food scraps make good compost.
3. Can you make compost out of scraps of polyester, metal, and plastic?	T	No. These are not things that naturally break down and rot when mixed with soil.

Strategies: Question-Answer Relationships *(cont.)*

Graphic Organizer

Code each question with one of these letters:

S = if the answer was stated

L = if you had to look for the answer

T = if you thought about it to come up with the answer; it wasn't in the text

Question	Code	Answer
1.		
2.		
3.		
4.		
5.		

Strategies: Envisioning Text

✛ Envisioning Text While Reading

Students who can visualize what's happening in text have a significant comprehension advantage. Promote these skills through think-alouds that describe your own visualization. Read aloud the first paragraph of a passage and describe the images that come to your mind. Be sure to include details that were not stated in the text (such as "the forest floor had splashes of sunlight where the sun filtered through the tree branches"). Then read the next two paragraphs and explain how you modified or added to your image based on the new information. For example, if later in the text you find out that it's raining, your sun-splashed forest floor has to change to soggy and dim.

When you are doing a think-aloud for your class, be sure to do the following:

◆ tell how your mental images relate to the passage's key concepts

◆ explain how your images help you to better understand the passage

◆ describe details, being certain to include those that you added from your own schema

◆ mention the use of your senses—the more the better

◆ show how the text affected your emotions

◆ discuss your empathy for the people or creatures in the text

◆ describe how your images change as you read further and gain more information

Sometimes students have difficulty visualizing the dimensions of unfamiliar things from the many facts and figures included in expository text. When you read a passage containing measurements, find ways for students to compare them to concrete things with which they are familiar. If a text reads, "A full-grown Komodo dragon can weigh 300 pounds and be six feet in length," your students may have difficulty picturing those dimensions. So gather together a group of about four students (each weighing 75–80 pounds) and have them stand in a tight knot in front of the class. Explain that their combined weight is about 300 pounds. Have students measure out six feet across the chalkboard or on the floor (use masking tape to mark the floor). These simple steps will give students a realistic idea of the size of the creature. For enormous dimensions (such as those of a dinosaur), mark the measurements with chalk on the school's driveway or parking lot.

Strategies: GIST; Supporting Details

✛ GIST: Finding the Main Idea

With the GIST strategy (Cunningham, 1982) students read a paragraph and immediately write its main idea in one sentence. To introduce this technique, key the information from a text on a paper, leaving an area after each paragraph in which the student can write the main idea sentence. After the students understand the procedure, have them read directly from a text, pausing after each paragraph to write a main idea sentence in a learning log. Here's an introductory example:

Australia's Great Barrier Reef, one of the seven natural wonders of the world, is the largest coral reef on Earth. Like most coral reefs, it lies just under the sea's surface. Coral reefs are created from living polyps that are attached to the reef. Living coral forms the top layer, built upon the bodies of ancestors from thousands of years ago. Scientists think that the Great Barrier Reef started forming about 500,000 years ago from the hardened skeletons of dead coral polyps.

Main idea: Australia's Great Barrier Reef, the largest coral reef on Earth, is formed by living coral polyps built upon the bodies of ancestors from long ago.

Coral polyps can be blue, green, purple, red, and yellow. They live together in gigantic colonies, giving the appearance of a sea garden. Each tiny coral polyp has a limestone skeleton. They attach themselves to each other with a flat sheet of tissue, then build up their skeletons by taking calcium from the water and using it to deposit calcium carbonate around the lower part of their bodies.

Main idea: The colorful coral polyps build up their limestone skeletons by removing calcium from the water and using it to deposit calcium carbonate around the lower part of their bodies.

✛ Finding the Main Idea and Supporting Details

To use this four-step strategy, begin with paragraphs in which the main idea is obvious, even if it is not stated in a topic sentence. The passages must be at students' independent reading level.

The Berlin Wall, built by the Communists in 1961, split the country of Germany in two. People on the east side of the Wall could no longer go to West Germany; people on the west side could no longer go to East Germany. The Wall was 20 feet high and made of solid concrete with barbed wire along the top. Soldiers, dogs, and guards in watchtowers kept people from crossing over the wall.

☞ **Step 1: Identify the key word(s) in each sentence.**
1. Berlin Wall, Communists, Germany
2. people on east side
3. people on west side
4. high, concrete, barbed wire
5. soldiers, dogs, watchtowers

☞ **Step 2: Identify the topic (what all the sentences have in common).**
The Berlin Wall

☞ **Step 3: Write a sentence stating the main idea (based on information from Steps 1 & 2).**
The Berlin Wall split Germany and kept apart the people on both sides.

☞ **Step 4: If possible, locate a sentence in the paragraph that states the main idea.**
"The Berlin Wall, built by the Communists in 1961, split the country of Germany in two."

Strategies: Pyramid

✤ Main Idea and Supporting Details: Pyramid

Just as a main idea is supported by facts, the top block of a pyramid is supported by the blocks beneath it. Students can graphically represent the main idea and the supporting details using the pyramid graphic organizer on page 53.

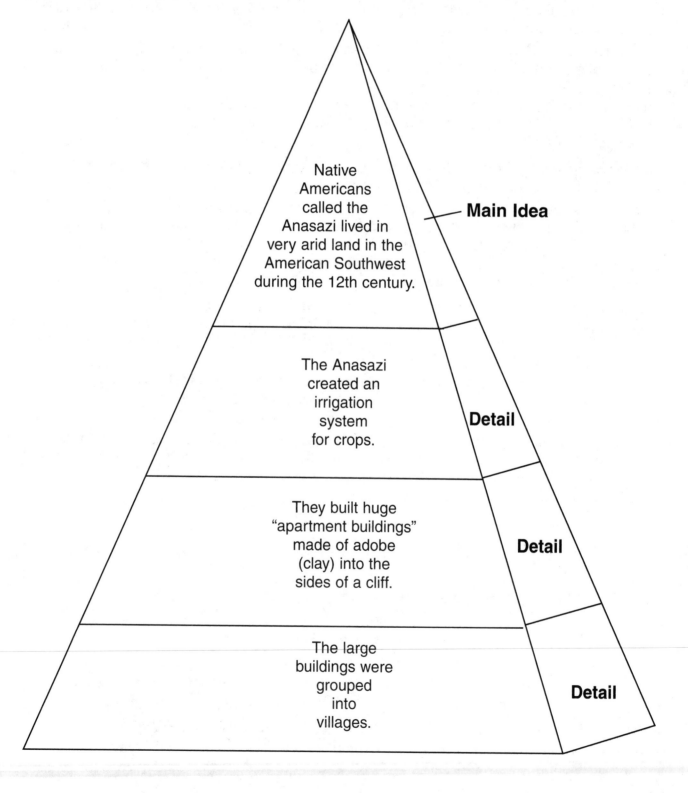

Strategies: Pyramid *(cont.)*

Graphic Organizer

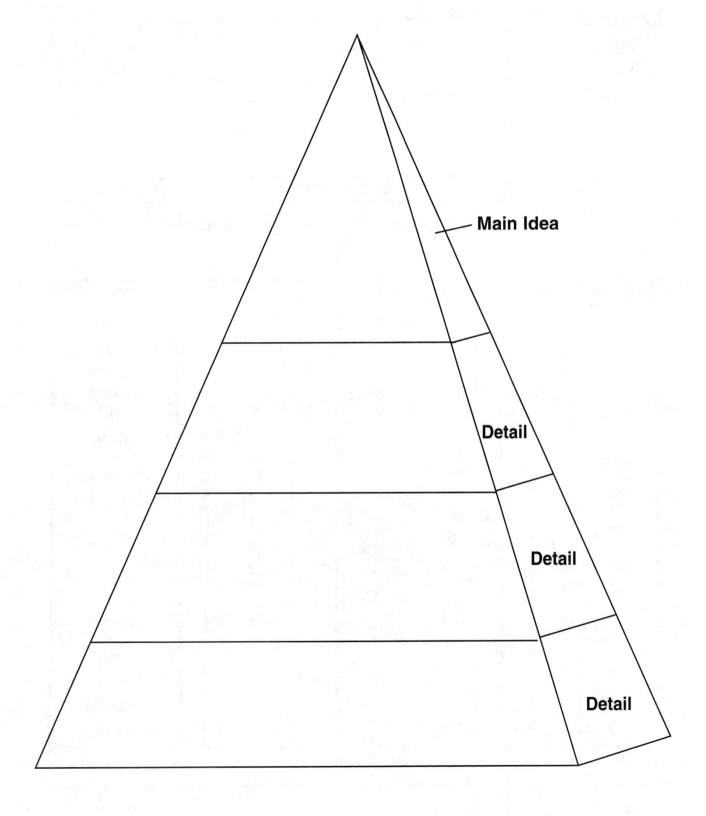

Strategies: Greek Temple

✛ **Main Ideas and Supporting Details: Greek Temple**

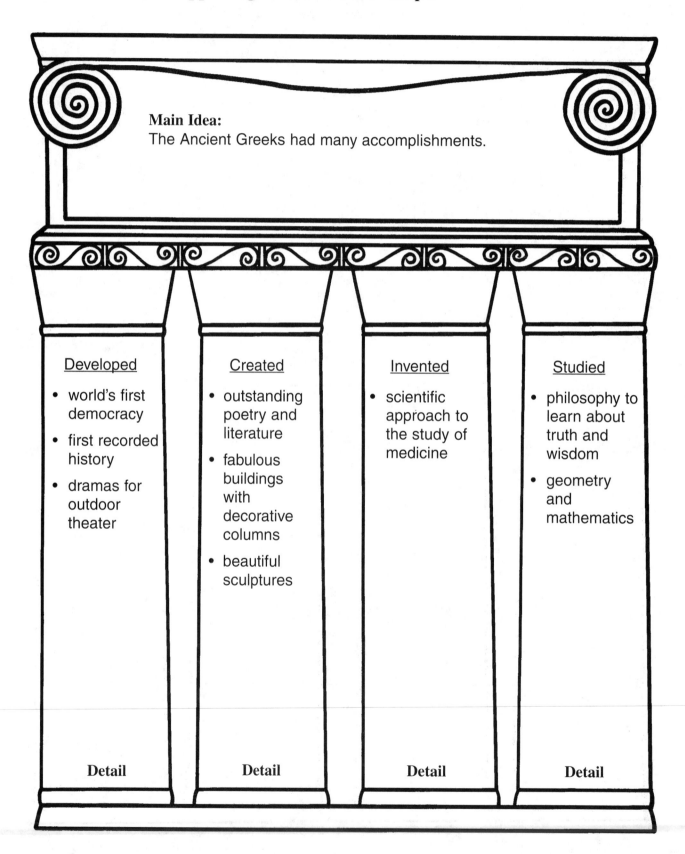

Main Idea:
The Ancient Greeks had many accomplishments.

Developed

- world's first democracy
- first recorded history
- dramas for outdoor theater

Created

- outstanding poetry and literature
- fabulous buildings with decorative columns
- beautiful sculptures

Invented

- scientific approach to the study of medicine

Studied

- philosophy to learn about truth and wisdom
- geometry and mathematics

Detail   **Detail**   **Detail**   **Detail**

Strategies: Greek Temple *(cont.)*

Graphic Organizer

Strategies: Inferential Skills; Signal Words

✤ Teaching Inferential Skills

To achieve success at reading nonfiction materials, your students need to use inferential skills. Teaching signal words is a good way for students to develop expository reading independence as well as strengthen their ability to monitor their own comprehension. Explain that authors expect readers to use their own experiences and knowledge as they read. They expect readers to "read between the lines" and understand things that are implied. To succeed with inferential comprehension, readers need to:

1. realize that inferences are tentative predictions that must be discarded if new information negates them
2. detect connotative language
3. recognize words that signal cause and effect or comparison relationships or a sequence of events
4. discern text structure and use it to construct meaning

✤ Signal Words

Concentrating on one type at a time, display or distribute a simple web with the text structure type named in the central circle with the signal words given in the chart below radiating out from it. Then choose an activity to build student awareness:

- Ask the students to point out the signal words in the materials you read as a class.
- Provide the class with sentences that have signal words and ask them to identify them.
- Make a word wall or bulletin board that groups the different types of signal words.
- Have the students read an expository passage. Then pass out a photocopy of the passage and ask students to highlight or underline the signal words in the material.
- Put the students into small groups and have each group create its own set of ten sentences that include signal words. Then ask a neighboring group to identify the signal words and what text structure they indicate.

These Signal Words	Indicate This Text Structure
since, because, caused by, as a result, before, after, so, therefore, thus, resulting in, so that, consequently, this led to, if/then, the consequences of which, when/then, the effects, leading up to, reasons, brought about, chief factors	**Cause & Effect** **Causes:** "Why did it happen?" **Effects:** "What happened?"
as well as, but, by contrast, compared with, in contrast to, related to, conversely, either/or, even if, even though, although, however, in spite of, instead, not only, unless, yet, on the other hand, all "-est" words: best, least, fewest, tallest, biggest, smallest, most, worst, etc.	**Compare/Contrast**
first, second, third, next, then, after, before, prior to, last, later, since that time, since then, now, while, meanwhile, at the same time, simultaneously, following, previously, finally, when, at last, in the end, on (date), at (time)	**Sequence**

56

Strategies: Text Structure

✛ Text Structure

Skillful readers use text structure to construct meaning. Guide your students through a sample text, emphasizing its organization. Demonstrate the main nonfiction text structures using a sentence about the concept of "taste" (as shown in the last column of the table):

Structure Type	Used To	Common Example	"Taste" Example
Description or Explanation	• define or describe a thing or concept	• encyclopedia entry about killer whales	• Taste is one of our five senses. Taste buds are tiny bumps on the human tongue that let us taste. Their purpose is to keep us from eating dangerous things.
Cause & Effect	• explain why or how something happens	• falling water generates electrical power	• When I put something in my mouth, my taste buds tell me whether I like it or not.
Sequence	• give a timetable of events over a period of time	• historical event or order in which things occur, such as the creation, use, and decline of the Erie Canal system	• First, a person chews the food. Then his taste buds send a signal to his brain about how the food tastes.
Lists	• state items—all with the same status/importance—with bullets or numbers	• directions on how to hook up a new VCR	• The five senses are sight, sound, touch, smell, and taste.
Compare/ Contrast	• show similarities and differences	• discuss positives and negatives of a changing to the metric system	• Unlike our other senses, taste is dependent upon our sense of smell.
Problem & Solution(s)	• identify what needs to be changed, improved, or eliminated and suggestion(s) of how to do so	• how to reduce the overpopulation of Canadian geese in the Northeast	• If the food tastes bad, I will spit it out.
Supported Opinion	• present a theory or opinion and give evidence or reasons for it	• conclusions drawn from research, results, studies (editorials, movie reviews)	• Some overweight people are so desperate to lose weight that they ask their doctor to destroy their sense of smell, rendering them unable to taste food. This is both dangerous and foolish. The sense of smell is necessary for safety reasons (such as smelling smoke or gas fumes). No one should rely on this drastic method for weight reduction.
Question & Answer	• pique interest	• frequently asked questions—a format seen often on the Internet	• Why do some people like anchovies while others don't? Because everyone's taste buds are unique.

Strategies: Stairstep Organizer

✣ Stairstep Organizer

When using the stairstep graphic organizer on page 59 to outline the order of an event, determine the climax and write it on the top step. Next, choose the three main events leading to the climax and put them on the steps on the left. Then choose the three main events after the climax and write them on the steps on the right. Remind students who are retelling a historical event that they need to attend to dates, times, and sequence signal words.

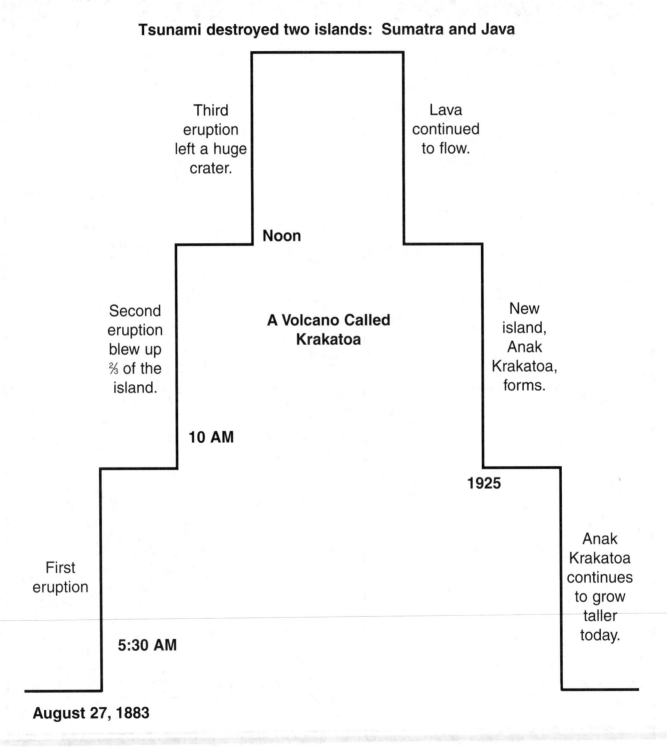

Tsunami destroyed two islands: Sumatra and Java

Third eruption left a huge crater.

Lava continued to flow.

Noon

Second eruption blew up ⅔ of the island.

A Volcano Called Krakatoa

New island, Anak Krakatoa, forms.

10 AM

1925

First eruption

Anak Krakatoa continues to grow taller today.

5:30 AM

August 27, 1883

Strategies: Stairstep Organizer *(cont.)*

Graphic Organizer

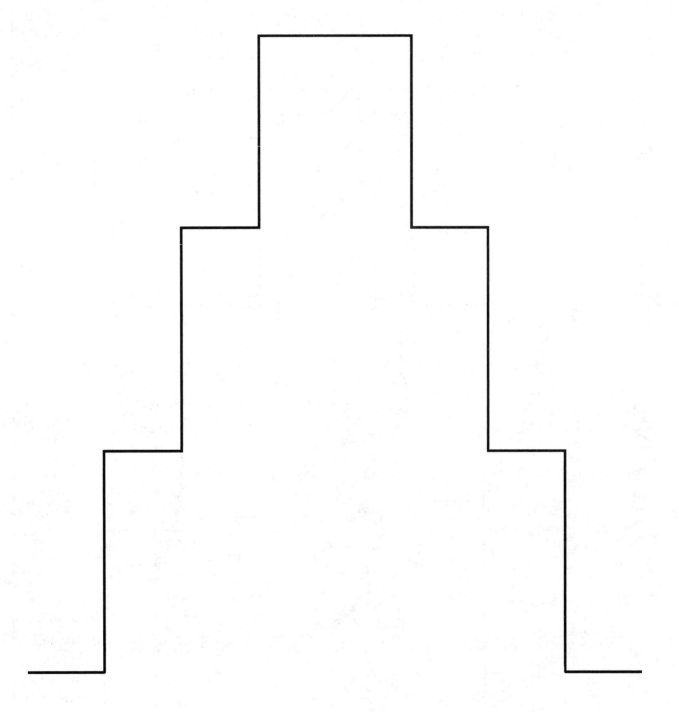

Strategies: Time Lines

❖ Time Lines

Creating time lines helps students to understand chronological order. Time lines are most often used to summarize the history of something (such as the Erie Canal), how an event unfolded (such as the Cuban Missile Crisis), or the significant events of an historical figure's life (such as Martin Luther King, Jr.).

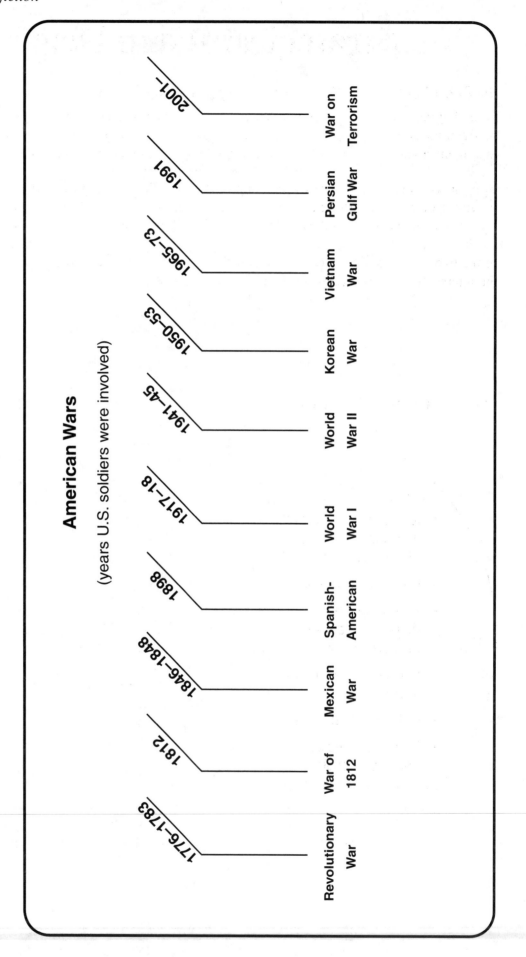

American Wars

(years U.S. soldiers were involved)

1776–1783	Revolutionary War
1812	War of 1812
1846–1848	Mexican War
1898	Spanish-American
1917–18	World War I
1941–45	World War II
1950–53	Korean War
1965–73	Vietnam War
1991	Persian Gulf War
2001–	War on Terrorism

Strategies: Venn Diagrams

✢ Two-Circle Venn Diagram

Venn diagrams have long been popular in helping students to ascertain the similarities and differences between ideas or things. Expository passages that have a theme supported by two specific examples lend themselves to the use of a Venn diagram, as shown in the example below.

You can visually demonstrate how a Venn diagram works by displaying an overhead of the graphic organizer on page 63. Place a yellow transparent circle over one circle. Explain what this circle represents. Remove the yellow circle. Next place a blue transparent circle over the other circle. Explain what this circle represents. Now put the yellow transparent circle back down. The intersection of the two circles will be green. Just as the color green is part yellow and part blue, the information in the intersection of the circles is a part of both circles.

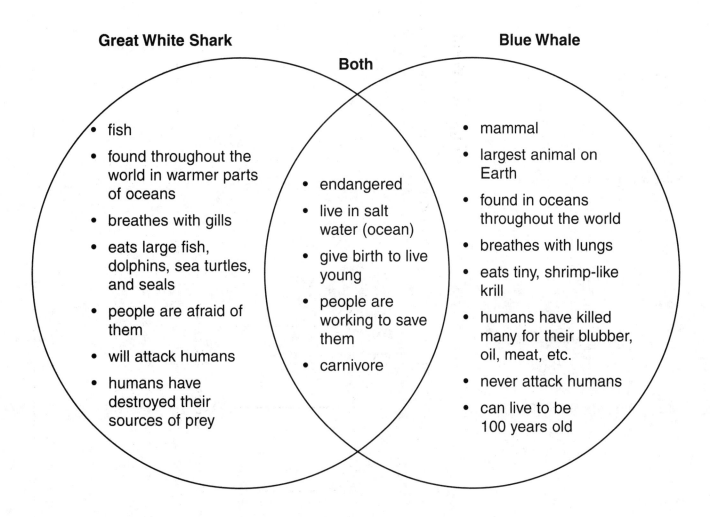

Great White Shark

Both

Blue Whale

- fish
- found throughout the world in warmer parts of oceans
- breathes with gills
- eats large fish, dolphins, sea turtles, and seals
- people are afraid of them
- will attack humans
- humans have destroyed their sources of prey

- endangered
- live in salt water (ocean)
- give birth to live young
- people are working to save them
- carnivore

- mammal
- largest animal on Earth
- found in oceans throughout the world
- breathes with lungs
- eats tiny, shrimp-like krill
- humans have killed many for their blubber, oil, meat, etc.
- never attack humans
- can live to be 100 years old

Strategies: Venn Diagrams *(cont.)*

⁘ Three-Circle Venn Diagram

After grade 5 you can use the three-circle Venn diagram on page 63 to compare and contrast three categories, resulting in some empty intersections. Visually demonstrate how a three-circle Venn diagram works by displaying an overhead of page 63. Place a yellow transparent circle over one circle and explain what this circle represents. Remove the yellow circle. Next, place a blue transparent circle over another circle and explain what this circle represents. Remove the blue circle. Put a red transparent circle over the third circle and explain what that circle represents. Now lay the yellow and blue transparent circles down. The intersection of the blue and yellow circles will be green. Just as the color green is part yellow and part blue, the information in the intersection of those circles is a part of both circles. The intersection of the red and yellow circles will be orange. Just as the color orange is part yellow and part red, the information in the intersection of those circles is a part of both circles. The intersection of the blue and the red circles will be purple. Just as the color purple is part blue and part red, the information in the intersection of those circles is a part of both circles. The intersection of all three circles will be dark brown (just as if you were mixing three colors of paint) and represents data that is applicable to all three categories. The following is an example:

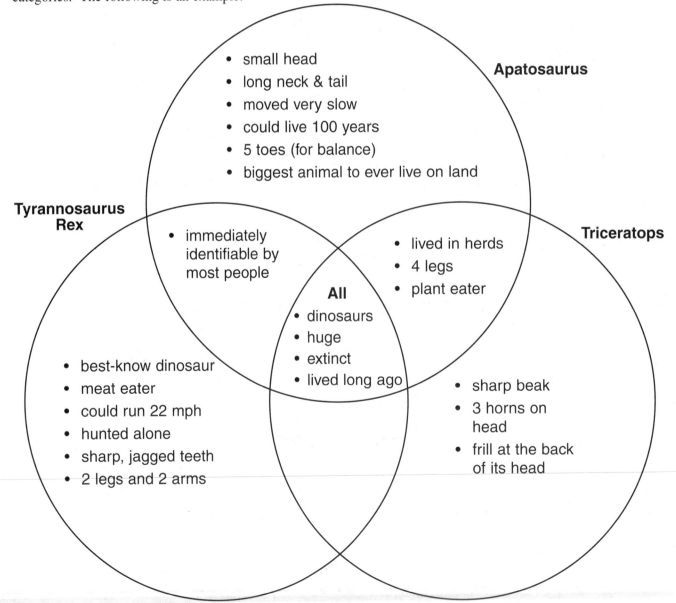

Apatosaurus
- small head
- long neck & tail
- moved very slow
- could live 100 years
- 5 toes (for balance)
- biggest animal to ever live on land

Tyrannosaurus Rex

- immediately identifiable by most people

- lived in herds
- 4 legs
- plant eater

Triceratops

All
- dinosaurs
- huge
- extinct
- lived long ago

- best-know dinosaur
- meat eater
- could run 22 mph
- hunted alone
- sharp, jagged teeth
- 2 legs and 2 arms

- sharp beak
- 3 horns on head
- frill at the back of its head

Strategies: Venn Diagrams

Graphic Organizers

Enlarge the following templates as needed.

Two-Circle Venn Diagram

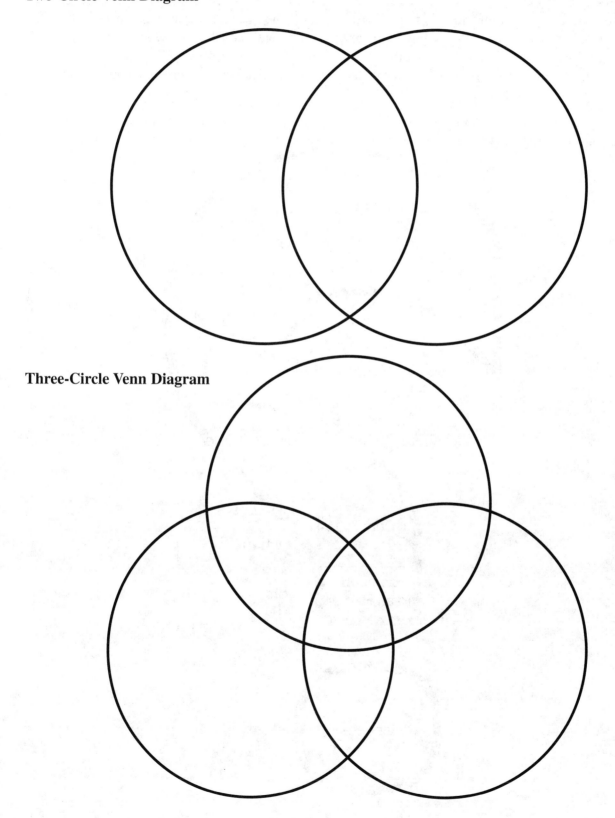

Three-Circle Venn Diagram

Strategies: Essential Questions

✥ Essential Questions

Use the Essential Questions graphic organizer to help your students pinpoint the key data in a passage. Use a photocopier to make an overhead transparency of page 65. After reading a nonfiction piece, ask the students to tell you what information to put in each part of the question for each sentence. Give your students additional practice by having them summarize several passages the whole class has already read. When you feel confident that the students understand the essential questions that should be answered in a summary, have them fill out the graphic organizer after they independently read expository text.

Example: On December 7, 1941, the Japanese bombed Pearl Harbor because they wanted to destroy American ships.

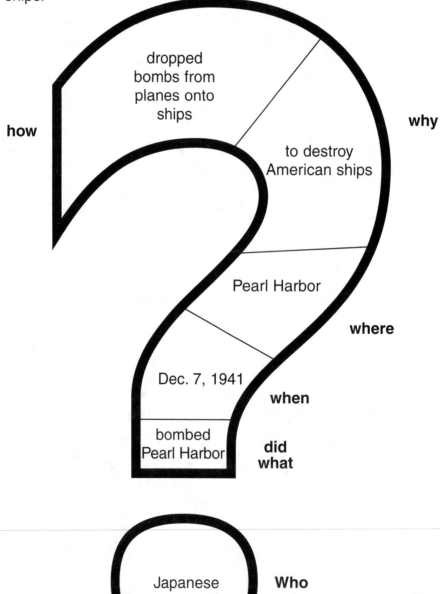

Strategies: Essential Questions *(cont.)*

Graphic Organizer

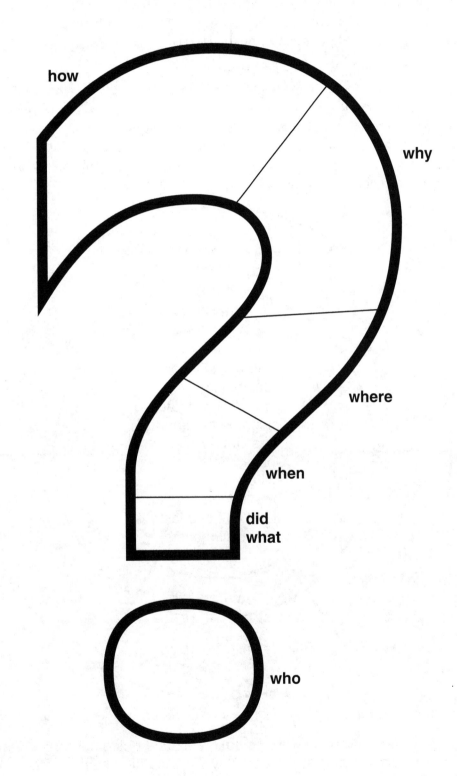

how

why

where

when

did
what

who

Strategies: Concept Wheel

✤ Concept Wheel

Show your students how to fill in the concept wheel on page 67. The entire passage's main idea goes in the center circle and the details from the whole passage that answer the questions radiate from the main idea like spokes on a wheel. Here is an example:

The Constitutional Convention was a meeting of state delegates to draft the United States Constitution. The delegates met in May 1787 in Philadelphia, Pennsylvania, to debate and vote on what would be included. Every state except Rhode Island sent representatives. The goal was to create a government by the people for the people. It took the men several months to iron out all the issues, but when they were done, they had a legal document that still influences our lives as Americans every single day. In the more than 200 years since the Convention, the Constitution has been amended many times, but its basic tenets of governmental checks and balances remains unchanged.

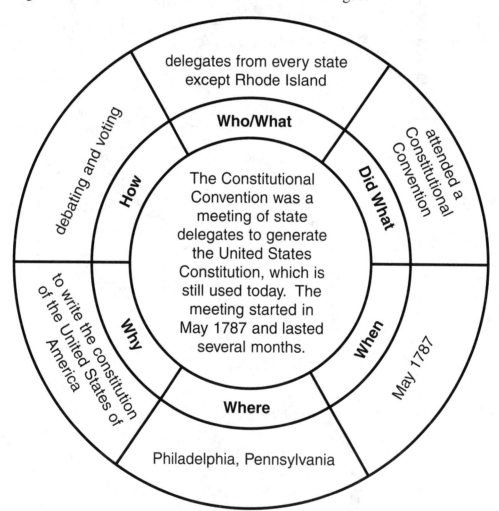

Use the information inside the wheel to write a short (three- or four-sentence) paragraph.

The Constitutional Convention was a meeting of state delegates to generate the United States Constitution, which is still used today. The meeting started in May 1787 and lasted several months. During that time the men debated and voted on the issues.

Strategies: Concept Wheel *(cont.)*

Graphic Organizer

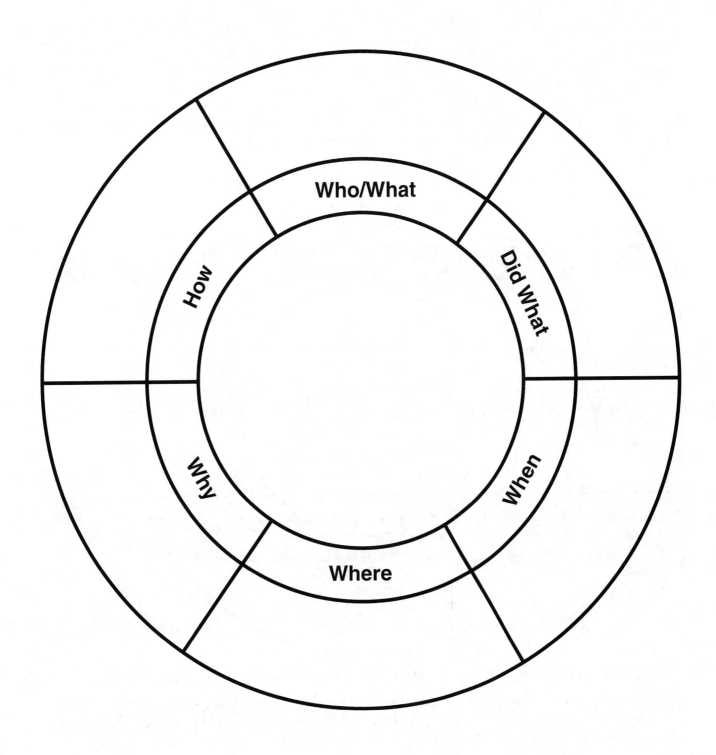

Strategies: Author's Motivation

✤ Examining the Author's Motivation

Authors write nonfiction to inform, to entertain, or to persuade. Fill out the graphic organizer on page 69 with your students after reading a nonfiction passage. Here is an example:

The ship *RMS Titanic* took three years to build. At the time it was the largest thing ever set in motion by humans. Built for the White Star Line, each of its four smokestacks could hold two train engines side by side. The ship was four city blocks long and 11 stories tall. It could carry 1,000 crew and 2,500 passengers.

In April 1912 the *Titanic* started on her first trip. Her owner, Bruce Ismay, and her captain, E.J. Smith, wanted the *Titanic* to set a speed record for crossing the Atlantic Ocean. Unfortunately, this helped to cause a terrible disaster that people still talk about today.

The Author's Motivation

To Inform Me	To Entertain Me	To Persuade Me
Example: The *Titanic* took three years to build. It was the largest thing ever set in motion. It had four gigantic smokestacks and was four city blocks long and 11 stories high. It could carry 3,500 people	**Example:**	**Example:**
Example: In April 1912 *Titanic* left England for NYC. The ship's owner and captain wanted it to set a speed record.	**Example:** Mentioned a terrible disaster that people are still talking about—makes me want to read to find out more.	**Example:**

Circle one of the following:

The author wrote this piece to (inform)   entertain   persuade   me.

Strategies: Author's Motivation *(cont.)*

Graphic Organizer

To Inform Me	To Entertain Me	To Persuade Me
Example:	Example:	Example:
Example:	Example:	Example:
Example:	Example:	Example:
Example:	Example:	Example:

Circle one of the following:

The author wrote this piece to   **inform**   **entertain**   **persuade**   me.

Introduction to Section 3: Discussing Nonfiction

Class discussions are critical to students' development of thinking skills. Listening to each other's ideas gives them a chance to consider varied ways of thinking and introduces them to different viewpoints. Discussions also help students to develop stronger reasoning skills by identifying underlying issues, defining problems clearly, debating about solutions or alternatives, and predicting the consequences of the alternatives. During discussions students develop important social skills, such as the following:

- taking turns
- encouraging others to participate
- valuing each other's ideas
- disagreeing with an idea without attacking the person who proposed it
- giving any group member full attention when he or she is speaking
- using others' ideas as a springboard for their own
- not dominating the discussion

Since students need experience with whole-group (pages 70–75), small-group (pages 76–79), and partner discussion (pages 80–83), the strategies listed in this section are divided accordingly.

Whole-Group Strategies: Class Observer; Emotions

✤ Class Observer

Class discussions should involve every child, so don't let one or a few students commandeer a discussion. Call on reticent pupils by name and ask what they think. Occasionally put students who tend to dominate class discussions in the role of "observer." Tell the observer that you need some help to come up with a discussion grade for the students. The observer does not participate in the discussion; instead he or she keeps track of who does the talking. Hand the observer a class list and ask him or her to make a check mark next to the name each time a student speaks. This is a subtle way to make the student aware of how some of their peers say a lot more than others and to consider his or her own behavior in future discussions.

✤ Discussing Emotions

Emotions are the most personal way to connect to text. Students will have a better understanding and retain more information when they try to empathize with those who lived through the event. For example, if you are reading about the Cherokee Trail of Tears, help your students to understand the emotional ramifications of the situation by asking questions such as these:

- How would you feel if an army came and said that everyone in your area must leave immediately and that the only things you could take would have to be carried 1,000 miles?
- What would you try to take with you?
- Could you carry those items 1,000 miles? (Show them how far away 1,000 miles is on a map.)
- How would you feel about leaving your home?
- Would you be afraid any of your family members couldn't walk that far?
- Would you be afraid that you couldn't walk that far?
- What feelings would you have about the new place where you are going to live?

Whole-Group Strategies: Both Sides; Taking a Stand; Visual Syntetics

⁜ Seeing It from Both Sides

Another way to help students connect emotionally with text is to read a passage about the same event written from two different points of view. This promotes the ability to look at a situation in more than one way, giving your students a well-rounded understanding of the information. For example, if you are reading about whalers hunting whales during the 1800s, read one version from the perspective of a whaler and the other from the perspective of a whale. Follow up with questions such as:

What emotions did you feel as a whaler? ⟶ What emotions did you feel as a whale?

What did you think when you saw the first whale? ⟶ What did you think when you first saw the ship?

How did you feel toward the whales? ⟶ How did you feel toward the whalers?

⁜ Taking a Stand

When you plan to study an issue that has two sides, post a sign on one side of the room stating one stance and a sign on the opposite wall stating the opposing stance. On a third wall post a sign labeled "Undecided." Have students select a sign to stand beneath. Do not state your own opinion, as students may be swayed by whatever you say. Students take turns holding a "talking stick" and explaining their opinions. The students may change their positions in the horseshoe if they are persuaded by a classmate's arguments. Anyone who speaks without holding the stick must sit down. Students must wait until a speaker signals that he or she is finished before raising their hands to get the stick. Each speaker must pass the stick to a student who holds the opposing view or who is undecided. Students will gain an appreciation for debate and enjoy the challenge of trying to persuade their peers to come to their side of the horseshoe.

⁜ Visual Syntetics

Visual syntetics (Crawley & Mountain, 1995) enhances higher-level thinking skills by having students relate a topic to a picture of an object that at first appears completely unrelated. Show the class a picture with no obvious relationship to the topic under study. Ask students to brainstorm what they see in the picture and how it could relate to the topic. Have students meet in small groups to discuss how they think the picture relates to the topic and each write a paragraph defending his or her opinion.

Since this is the epitome of synthesizing skills, visual syntetics should be done as a group activity. Here's a visual syntetics example: Your class has been studying about the human circulatory system. You bring in a picture of the plumbing (pipes) inside a building. The relationship you want students to see is that pipes can get clogged if the wrong things (food, fats, hair) are put down the drain—just as arteries get clogged if a person eats a lot of the wrong (high-cholesterol) things.

Whole-Group Strategies: Questioning the Author

❖ Questioning the Author

The Questioning the Author strategy (Beck, et al., 1997) was specifically designed to help students take an active, questioning attitude toward text. Using this method, the text sparks queries, which in turn stimulate class discussion. The teacher guides the discussion to promote a shared construction of ideas and concepts by students. This discussion happens during the course of the reading so that students cooperatively derive meaning from a text.

The emphasis is on queries rather than questions. Students taught through the use of queries tend to integrate ideas more readily across texts and content areas than those taught with traditional questioning methods. Queries also make struggling students less resistant to reading nonfiction.

What's the difference between questions and queries? Traditional classroom questions have literal, find-it-stated-in-the-text answers. Since such questions do not require that students to analyze information or do anything new with it, it's little wonder that so few remember what they have read. In contrast, queries require students to *process* information.

Traditional Questions	Questioning-the-Author Queries
Students find answers in the text and use the author's words to state the answer.	Students have to think about the information and respond in their own words.
Students view text as an infallible place to find correct answers.	Students view text as a reference for correct answers.
mostly one-on-one teacher-to-student interactions	more student-to-student interaction

Here are the steps in a Questioning the Author lesson:

1. Arrange the classroom desks into a U-shape so that students can easily see and interact with each other.

2. Teach your students to view authors as fallible. This means that the students acknowledge that some expository writers may not research a topic thoroughly, express his or her ideas clearly, or explain that something is just a theory.

3. Plan the Questioning the Author lesson by reading the text to determine for yourself the major concepts you want students to understand. Anticipate and plan for potential problems by predicting how the ideas in the text might be interpreted (or misinterpreted). You can do this by noticing whenever you are doing extra work—having to reread for clarity or stopping to think about how one idea relates to another. If an experienced reader like you hesitates, your students will falter there, too.

Whole-Group Strategies: Questioning the Author *(cont.)*

✣ Questioning the Author *(cont.)*

4. Segment the text by deciding on specific stopping points where you will initiate queries and class discussion.

5. Establish queries for each segment. Queries should be open-ended and put the onus for developing understanding on the students. Typical queries include the following:

   ◆ What does the writer mean by _____ ?

   ◆ What is the writer's message?

   ◆ What is the writer thinking?

   ◆ What is the writer trying to say?

   ◆ What is the writer's purpose in telling us this?

   ◆ Why did the writer choose this presentation?

   ◆ Did the writer explain this clearly?

   ◆ Does this agree with what we read before?

   ◆ How does this connect with what the writer has already said?

   ◆ Why do you think the writer chose to include this information?

   ◆ What did the writer assume we already know?

   ◆ Is the writer biased? How do you know?

6. Read the text aloud with the students, stopping at the designated points, stating a query and guiding student discussion. Your role is to initiate and facilitate the discussion.

7. During discussions you may reiterate the key points from a student's contribution in another way (in case someone in the class didn't understand). You want your students to see you as a learner who asks questions, too. So it is a good idea to occasionally deflect student questions addressed to you back to the class, especially those that you feel that the students can effectively answer. However, if your students appear to be missing a major point or seem incapable of grasping an idea on their own, make the point by modeling it as your own thinking: "The author seems to be saying that the colonists were very afraid of minor injuries. Maybe it's because they didn't have antibiotics back then. Without antibiotics even minor cuts that got infected could become deadly."

Whole-Group Strategies: Discussion Prompts

✥ Discussion Prompts

After reading or listening to nonfiction material, choose a set of discussion prompts (Zarnowski, 1998) that are appropriate to the specific passage and use them in a whole-class discussion.

What's the main idea? supporting details?

- ✦ What did you do to find the main idea? the supporting details?
- ✦ What strategies do you use to locate the main idea when it is not stated?
- ✦ Who can summarize this passage?
- ✦ What steps did you follow to prepare the summary?
- ✦ What strategies do you use to prepare a summary?
- ✦ Did you find summarizing this passage simple or hard? Why?

How can we differentiate between facts and opinions?

- ✦ What facts did the author provide in the article?
- ✦ What opinions did the author give in the article?
- ✦ Did the author effectively distinguish between fact and opinion?
- ✦ How do we know which statements are facts?
- ✦ What is the author's opinion of this topic? How do you know?
- ✦ Did the author's attitude affect the way the facts and opinions were presented?
- ✦ Was the author's interpretation of the data correct? Explain your reasoning.

How can we differentiate between relevant and irrelevant information?

- ✦ What is the evidence?
- ✦ Is the evidence credible? How does the author know?
- ✦ Is the evidence provided relevant?
- ✦ How are the things, people, or events connected?
- ✦ What caused _____ ?
- ✦ What were the consequences of _____ ?

What's the value in knowing history?

- ✦ What is the value of knowing this information?
- ✦ Does it help us to understand another time or place?
- ✦ Does it help to us to understand related events?
- ✦ Does this remind you of anything else that we've studied?
- ✦ Could something similar happen to you or to someone you love?
- ✦ How does this apply to [a situation] today?

Whole-Group Strategies: Discussion Prompts *(cont.)*

How are historical accounts pieced together?

- ◆ Do other sources support the author's information or ideas?
- ◆ What sources were chosen? Why were they used?
- ◆ What conflicting evidence did the author find?
- ◆ Which account or details do you find most believable? Why? (Use this question after reading conflicting accounts or when the author explains several theories and leaves the reader to choose his or her own interpretation.)
- ◆ What conclusions were reached?

How can we better understand an historical figure?

- ◆ What challenges did he or she face?
- ◆ What brought about these challenges?
- ◆ What did he or she do to overcome the challenges?

Why does the author offer this specific interpretation?

- ◆ Why does the author write this?
- ◆ For whom is this written (audience)?
- ◆ What sources is chosen? Why were they used?
- ◆ Is the author's perspective logical?
- ◆ How well does the author support his or her premise?
- ◆ Do other authors agree with the conclusions reached?
- ◆ Do other readers agree with the conclusions reached?
- ◆ Do you agree with the author?
- ◆ What do you disagree with the author about?
- ◆ What would you like to ask the author?
- ◆ What does the author want us remember?

What's the purpose of connotative language?

- ◆ Are there any words or sentences that make you react strongly? Which ones? What is your reaction?
- ◆ What images come to mind as you read this passage? Which words or sentences caused those images?
- ◆ What is the author's opinion of this topic? How do you know?
- ◆ Who is the author's intended audience? How does this affect the author's tone?
- ◆ Does the author include only negative facts? Only positive ones?
- ◆ What conclusions are reached? Do you agree with these conclusions?

Is the author giving a hypothesis or making a prediction?

- ◆ What was the author's hypothesis or prediction?
- ◆ Does the author say that he or she is certain or making an educated guess?
- ◆ Which of the author's statements are supported? Which are unsupported?
- ◆ Is the author's interpretation of the data correct?
- ◆ Do you agree with the author's conclusion?
- ◆ Do other authors agree with these conclusions? Do other readers?

Small-Group Discussion Methods

These are the essential components of small cooperative group instruction:

1. Groups work best when three to four heterogeneous students are put into each team. On a team of three, that means one high-performing student, one average student, and one low-performing student. In a team of four, two of the students would be average. Do not enlarge the teams; research has established that the fewer the group members, the more each individual participates.

2. Students know that the members of the group are dependent on each other. Thus, the success of each teammate relies upon the success of all.

3. Everyone must do his or her share. This includes helping teammates as well as demonstrating knowledge of the materials.

4. Since some students learn best by talking things through with their peers, provide opportunities for plenty of interaction among teammates.

5. Students need instruction in the social skills listed in the introduction to this section (page 70). They must use these skills to effectively interact with their teammates.

You act as a facilitator by:

- ensuring that each member does a specified task or a portion of the overall task
- having students adopt specific roles, such as facilitator, scribe, timekeeper, etc.
- providing only one set of materials to each group to encourage interaction
- requiring that students talk quietly to keep the noise level in the room to a minimum
- circulating among the groups, offering encouragement, resolving disputes, and gently guiding students in the formation of essential interpersonal skills.

Small-Group Strategies: Facts and Opinions; Brainstorming Carousel

❖ Discussing Facts and Opinions

Make photocopies of expository material containing both facts and opinions. Have students underline facts with one color marker and opinions with another color marker, then form groups of three and discuss what they've underlined and why.

❖ Brainstorming Carousel

After reading expository text, try a brainstorming carousel by posting six sheets of chart or butcher paper around the room. On each sheet, put a simple question: Who? Did What? When? Where? Why? How? Put the students into six groups and assign each group to one of the question sheets. Each group has two minutes to write its ideas for its question on the sheet before it rotates clockwise to the next question sheet. Then each group has three minutes to read what has already been written on the sheet and add its own unique contributions. This continues until the groups have rotated through all six questions. For example, after studying the Revolutionary War, the first group that stands in front of the "who" sheet writes American colonists. Then the second group reads what has been written and adds the British and the king to the same sheet. After that, the third group reads the sheet and decides to write redcoats and minutemen on the page, while the fourth group adds Whigs and Tories. The fifth group puts the Continental Army and George Washington, etc.

Small-Group Strategies: Roundtable Discussions; Achievement Teams

✛ Roundtable Discussions

Roundtable discussions (Parker, 2001) work best with groups of three. One student takes the role of the facilitator by keeping the discussion moving and making sure everyone has an opportunity to voice an opinion. Another student takes the role of scribe and records important points. A third student acts as timekeeper, moving the group through the task in a timely manner. Roundtable discussions work by starting with the facilitator stating a topic and his or her opinion, then moving around the table clockwise and having each student do the same. Students must listen courteously, disagree appropriately, and challenge others' statements that appear to be contrary to the facts. Roundtable discussions are particularly effective for:

◆ talking about current events

◆ planning a major class activity (such as organizing an assembly or a show)

◆ critiquing a film, video, or other audiovisual presentation

◆ debating a school or community issue (such as, How can we help those in our city who are hungry?). As a follow up, reconvene as a whole group. List the options on the board, overhead, or chart paper and have the class vote on what they want to do.

✛ Student Achievement Teams

Teaching something to another person makes you learn it more thoroughly yourself. Student Achievement Teams, an adaptation of Information Intermix (Capuzzi, 1973), puts each student into the role of a teacher.

1. Form groups of three.

2. Give each student a specific part of the chapter to read and learn.

3. Students spend a designated amount of time (set by you) independently reading and learning their portion.

4. The students meet with their teams to teach others in the group about the materials read. The first student teaches group members about the first part of the material; the rest of the group listens and takes notes. Next, the second student teaches about the next portion of the material, and so on. Each group member will be a teacher once and a listener twice.

5. The entire class reconvenes for discussion and to ask questions of the teacher.

6. When you feel that the class has sufficient knowledge, announce a test.

7. Individual test scores are recorded for each student and used in each student's overall course grade.

8. The test scores of the students in each group are also averaged to obtain a group grade, which is also a component of each student's overall course grade.

Small-Group Strategies: Jigsaw

❖ Jigsaw

Some teachers prefer the Jigsaw (Slavin, 1980) method of cooperative learning. This method differs from Student Achievement Teams in three ways:

- ✦ All students read all the material before receiving a specific section to study and prepare to teach.

- ✦ Members of each team work first with people from other teams before teaching the members of their own team.

- ✦ Only individual scores are given for tests.

Here's how it works:

1. Read the text in advance and determine the appropriate division of the material.

2. All of the students read the entire chapter.

3. Students form teams with no more than four members.

4. You announce the divisions of the material. (For example, you may specify pages 378–381 as section one; pages 382–386 as section two, and pages 387–392 as section three.)

5. The teams themselves assign these sections, one to each team member.

6. Section one group members from all of the different teams meet to discuss their material and, in essence, become "experts" who will teach the material to their home teams. Meanwhile, section two group members from all teams meet with each other. The same goes for the students in charge of learning section three.

7. Home teams reconvene with all their members. Each teammate spends time teaching other group members, and in turn, learning from other group members.

8. Everyone takes an exam and earns individual scores, which are a component of each student's overall course grade.

Small-Group Strategies: Collaborative Reading; Readers' Guild

❖ Collaborative Strategic Reading

Collaborative strategic reading (Klingner & Vaughn, 1998) is a group activity in which students take on specific roles as they preview, read, discuss, and summarize an informational text. This technique gives the students a real sense of control over their own education and works well in inclusive classrooms that have students with learning disabilities or English-as-a-second-language learners.

Put students into groups of three. Have each group preview the passage together for two to three minutes, paying special attention to the who, what, when, where, why, and how. The group members then take turns reading the text aloud to each other, stopping to discuss words or concepts that they don't understand. Assign each student a role in the group (after they are used to this activity, they can select their own roles). The leader guides the preview and discussion and jots down any words that stump anyone in the group during the reading. The summarizer helps the group to paraphrase each paragraph in the passage. The recorder writes down group-generated possible test questions that will be submitted to the teacher.

After reading, the groups must restate the most important idea for each paragraph in a dozen words or less, resulting in a paraphrase for every paragraph in the passage. The students then use these summary statements to write one question for each paragraph on a card. The questions should be ones that they think might be asked on a test and cannot have simple yes/no answers. Once the groups have formulated their questions, choose one of these three options:

1. Have each group select the one best question it generated and pass it to another group to see if its members can answer it.

2. Ask each group to select its one best question and write it on the board or overhead. Have everyone in the class copy the questions and answer them as a homework assignment.

3. Collect all the questions and use them to write a quiz; this will result in the students feeling empowered and thoroughly involved in the evaluation process.

❖ Readers' Guild

Establish an extracurricular or after-school group (such as a readers' guild) in which students read books on a specified nonfiction subject and come ready to discuss the topic at a monthly meeting. This is a valuable way for students to interact across grade levels. You can involve the librarian by having him or her display a set of relevant nonfiction books in a specified area of the library. This makes it easy for students who participate in Readers' Guild to select a book quickly.

Partner Strategies: Features; Simulations; Interactive Guide

✢ What Are the Features of Nonfiction Works?

Have students work with partners to "discover" nonfiction books' features and to establish the kinds of information various nonfiction resources contain. Have the pairs analyze the phone book, encyclopedia, almanac, dictionary, *Guinness World Book of Records*, thesaurus, atlas, reference works, nonfiction picture books, catalogs, trade books, magazines, posters, etc. Extend this activity by giving the pairs a list of things to be found and asking what reference source students would check first. For example, ask where to look to find the height of the tallest building in the world.

✢ Computer Simulations

Interactive computer simulations that promote learning and discussion and can be done in pairs include *The Oregon Trail*; *The Amazon Trail*; *Decisions, Decisions*; *Where in the World Is Carmen Sandiego?*; *Where in Time Is Carmen Sandiego?*; and *Where in the USA Is Carmen Sandiego?*

✢ Interactive Reading Guide

An Interactive Reading Guide (Wood, 1988) is especially good for math problems, although it can be used for any type of text. Read through a selection to prepare a set of coded directions, using this code:

$\triangle$**A** = do this alone   **P** = do with a partner

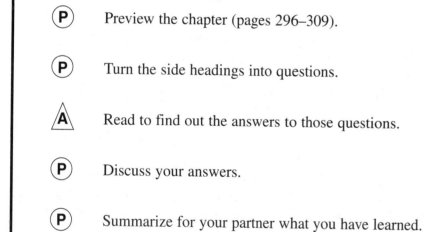

Here's an example:

P   Preview the chapter (pages 296–309).

P   Turn the side headings into questions.

A   Read to find out the answers to those questions.

P   Discuss your answers.

P   Summarize for your partner what you have learned.

A   Work through problems 1–5 on page 310.

P   Discuss answers to problems 1–5.

Partner Strategies: Summary Grid

✛ Summary Grid

After studying a subject, copy (and, if necessary, enlarge) the Summary Grid Graphic Organizer below. Write the main category down the edge and two specifics across the top. Give a time limit for student pairs to fill the squares with a word or phrase that starts with that letter and fits the category. The following is an example:

	Revolutionary	Civil
W	**W**ashington was the leader of the Continental Army	**W**ithdrawal of southern states from the Union to form their own nation
A	**A**gainst the British	**A**ppommatox Courthouse—Lee surrendered to Grant
R	**R**edcoats were worn by the British infantry	**R**ebelling states were called the Confederate States of America
S	**S**urrender by British in 1783 in Paris	**S**lavery was outlawed as a result of the war

- -

Graphic Organizer

Directions: Write a word or a phrase that begins with the given letter and relates to the topic.

Partner Strategies: Why? Pie

⁘ Why? Pie

The Why? Pie strategy (Bromley, et al., 1999) encourages students to identify essential relationships between objects or concepts. Model the strategy by reading aloud an expository passage and then asking questions that begin with the word "why" and can only be answered by inference (the answer is not directly stated in the article). Have the students finish reading the passage and work in pairs to come up with why questions about the material, putting one question in each section of the Why? Pie. They should also discuss possible responses to their questions. After that they can exchange questions with another pair and develop responses to those questions as well.

Here's an example of a student's Why? Pie after reading this article:

Grasslands cover one-fourth of Earth's land surface. Grasslands, or prairies, are covered by grass. Few trees grow there. Grasslands are usually found on the inside of continents on flat ground. They usually lie between deserts and forests. Every continent except Antarctica has some grasslands. All over the world many grasslands have been cultivated.

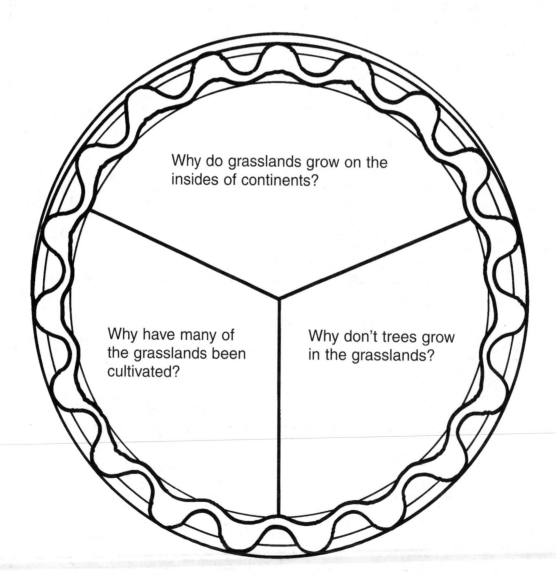

Why do grasslands grow on the insides of continents?

Why have many of the grasslands been cultivated?

Why don't trees grow in the grasslands?

Partner Strategies: Why? Pie *(cont.)*

Graphic Organizer

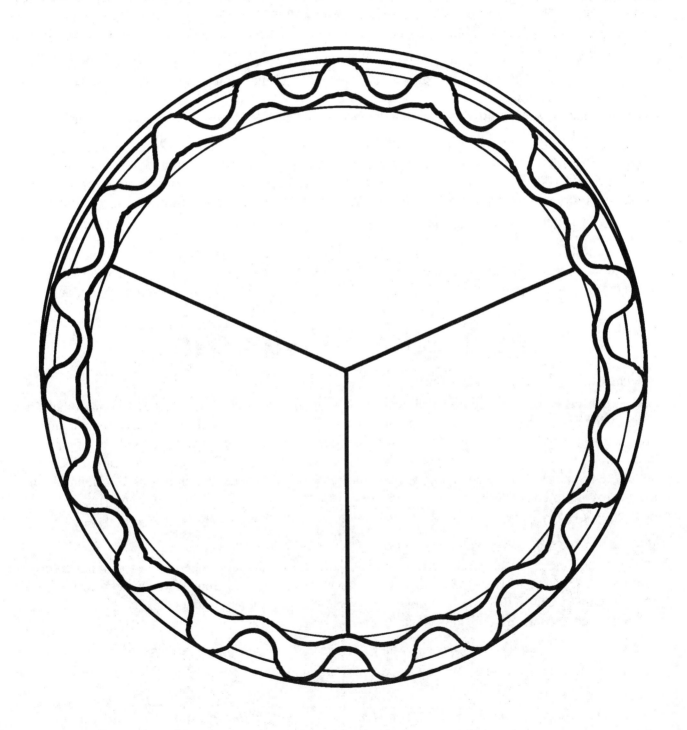

Introduction to Section 4: Listening to Nonfiction

The school environment demands that students have good listening skills; indeed, listening permeates every facet of the academic curriculum. In addition, effective listening skills yield substantial reading comprehension benefits. Thus, students need to be good listeners in order to understand, take adequate notes, and remember information they hear.

Since the ability to take notes while listening is critical for success in high school and college, the development of these skills needs to begin early in a student's educational career. Taking notes promotes active listening; and the cognitive processes associated with hearing, comprehending, and writing provides the best reinforcement of material. The strategies in this section develop your students' note taking skills through the use of informal outlines and graphic organizers.

A student's listening level is the level at which he or she can comprehend material read or spoken aloud. Typically a person's listening level is approximately two years above his or her reading level. It is crucial that students of all ages hear informational text read aloud in order to increase their knowledge of language structure, improve writing skills, and introduce new vocabulary in context.

While careful listening is an important goal, use closed captioning whenever available during videos, films, etc. This helps students with minor hearing impairments and speakers of English as a second language, as well as provides support to those who feel overwhelmed by information presented aurally.

Strategies: Visualizing

✛ Visualizing While Listening

Like reading, listening is a receptive skill that relies upon visualization skills. Listening comprehension is like seeing a movie in the mind. When you introduce this skill, start with fiction because students have had the most experience with this genre. Ask your students to close their eyes and keep them closed throughout the exercise. If students find that impossible, offer blindfolds. Start out with only one or a few sentences at a time, stopping frequently to guide the visualization process. Emphasize that the students are to consider the questions, not answer them aloud. In the following transcript, the italicized words are the text, and inside the quotes are what the teacher said.

Once upon a time long, long ago, a king and queen lived in a castle.

"Picture the castle. What else is nearby? Now see the king. What does he look like? What color are his eyes? his hair? Is he old or young? handsome or ugly? fat or thin? What is he wearing? Now see the queen. What does she look like? What color are her eyes and hair? Is she old or young? pretty or ugly? fat or thin? What is she wearing?"

The king and the queen were very rich, but they were very sad because they had no children.

"Look at the king and queen. What is the expression on his face? on her face? Why are those expressions there?"

The king feared that he would have no heir and that upon his death the kingdom would fall into the hands of his wicked cousin, Walter.

"What does Walter look like? What color are his eyes? his hair? Is he old or young? handsome or ugly? fat or thin? What is he wearing?"

Strategies: Visualizing *(cont.)*

After the class has heard the story in this manner, each student must have the opportunity to respond to at least one question that was not answered in the text, such as the following:

- ◆ How tall was the king? the queen?
- ◆ Is the king fat or thin? How about the queen?
- ◆ What color hair does the king have? the queen have?
- ◆ What color eyes does the king have? the queen have?
- ◆ Are the stones of the castle gray or brown? Does it have towers? a drawbridge?
- ◆ What is near the castle?

Your students may protest, "But the author didn't tell us that." Explain that that's not what's important—what did they see when they heard it? Stress that good listeners form "a movie in their minds" by blending information from the text with their own background knowledge.

Next, read aloud a nonfiction text and encourage students to incorporate their prior knowledge as they imagine the scene. When you've finished, discuss what they saw in their minds. For example, after you read "Woodchucks live in burrows in fields," stop and ask the students to picture the field. Then ask questions that can only be answered through visualization:

- ◆ What is growing in the field? Is there tall grass? trees? What kinds? Farm crops? What kinds? Flowers? What kinds? Weeds? What kinds?
- ◆ What season is it?
- ◆ What sounds do you hear in the field?
- ◆ Can you smell anything?
- ◆ What is nearby?
- ◆ Is this a field that you've actually seen somewhere? Where?

Finally, walk your students through a nonfiction piece asking them to imagine the scene using all of their senses (Rose, 1989). For example, if you are going to read about the Battle of Lexington, have the students close their eyes as you read:

The first battle of the Revolutionary War was fought in Lexington in 1775.

"Think of pictures of war that you have seen. In 1775 did either country have tanks? machine guns? bombs? What are they holding in their hands? What will they fight with?"

The first shot was fired on an April morning at a wooden bridge. The colonists were on one side of the bridge and the British on the other.

"Picture the wooden bridge. Hear the brook as it flows under the bridge. Feel the warm spring sun. Hear the birds twittering in the trees. See the trained army on one side of the bridge. See the men all dressed in bright red coats with brass buttons. See the group of men on the other side. They are farmers dressed in plain cotton shirts and work pants with suspenders."

Continue to work your way through the text in this manner. When you have finished, put the students into groups of three and ask them to collaboratively draw three images that show how they envisioned the beginning, middle, and end. First the group members should discuss and decide what three images they will draw. Then they should divide the work, with each student doing one of the drawings. Finally, they should label each other's illustrations with a sentence or caption.

Strategies: Film Discussion; Voice; Points of View

❖ Film Discussion

View a film and determine four or five good stopping points. Then put students into groups of three. Give each group member a number 1–3. Show a portion of the film. Stop at the first predetermined stopping point. The students have three minutes in which to discuss and student number one to record what the group feels is the key idea. Continue in this manner, rotating the job of scribe to the next student number every time you stop the film.

❖ Voice

To show how voice affects a composition, read aloud several short nonfiction selections, some written in first and others written in third person. Ask the students: From whose viewpoint are we hearing this? How do you know? Brainstorm a list of advantages and disadvantages for writing in both the first and third person.

❖ Listening to Different Points of View

Help students to learn that articles are written from different points of view and for different purposes. Just think of how—depending upon who the writer is—the points of view would differ on Christopher Columbus, Malcolm X, and Betty Friedman. Highlight the concept of point of view by reading aloud any version of the classic "The Three Little Pigs," followed by John Scieszka's *The True Story of the Three Little Pigs* (Viking, 1999). Follow these readings with these critical thinking questions:

◆ How would it have changed the piece if the writer had used the other voice?

◆ Why do you think the two versions of the same story are so different?

◆ What effect does having a different narrator have on the stories?

86

Strategies: Note Taker; Enabling Questions; Listen-Read-Discuss

✛ Class Note Taker

After you have taught the class how to take notes from an oral presentation, you can use this strategy. Give students turns being the class note taker. When you are reading aloud, speaking, or the class is watching a film or guest presenter, one designated student takes notes. Photocopy these notes and distribute them to the class. Each student can then individually highlight or add his or her own notes to the copies. At the beginning of the next class, read aloud the notes and, if necessary, have the class members add to them. Then present new material while a new note taker works as the class scribe. This continues until every student in the class has had the opportunity to be the note taker. The exposure to a wide variety of note taking styles lets students know that there is more than one way to take good notes.

✛ Enabling Questions

Enabling Questions (Manzo & Manzo, 1997) promote active listening during a lecture.

1. Write each of the questions listed below on a separate card.

2. Randomly distribute the cards to your class members.

3. Tell these students to raise their hands and ask the question on the card at any time that they feel is appropriate during your lecture. Such interruptions in a lecture often reactivate the entire group of students' listening and attention when it may have begun to wander.

"What is most often misunderstood about the information you are presenting to us?"	"If we could only remember one thing from this lecture, what should it be?"	"Does anyone disagree with this information? What is their stance?"

✛ Listen-Read-Discuss

The Listen-Read-Discuss strategy (Manzo & Casale, 1985) uses multiple intelligences to strengthen students' comprehension of expository text.

Step 1—Listen: First, present a brief oral summary of the material.

Step 2—Read: Allow students to read the material, either to themselves or aloud.

Step 3—Discuss: When they have finished, have students set the reading aside. Ask these questions:

   ✦ "What do you understand about what you just read?"

   ✦ "What don't you understand about what you just read?"

   ✦ "What questions do you still have about this subject?"

Strategies: Fact and Opinion; Persuasive Language

✛ Differentiating Between Facts and Opinions

Students must listen critically to assess the truth and relevance of information. Be sure that they understand that facts are as follows:

- ✦ a number of things observed

- ✦ actions that can be observed

- ✦ physical features of a thing or a person

- ✦ words specifically written or said by someone (it's a fact that they said or wrote that information). Of course, what was said or written may be an opinion.

Only inferences can be made about the following:

- ✦ the feelings, motives, or personalities of others

- ✦ the future

- ✦ another person's intended meaning

Students also need to recognize facts stated with connotative language. One of the best places to show students facts interspersed with connotative language is sports reporting. Ask the students to listen to a television sports report, and they will find out that teams don't win, they "batter" and "trounce." The losing team doesn't just lose, it gets "destroyed" or "slammed." Point out that the final score, the name of the winning person or team, and the names of the losing person or team are all facts imbedded in a lot of rhetoric.

✛ Recognizing Persuasive Language

Persuasive prose contains words that the author uses to evoke specific feelings in the readers. For example, during a radio commercial a travel agent might say, "The Dominican Republic is a jewel glittering in the Caribbean Sea"—which is a far cry from the meteorologist's radio report, "The Dominican Republic lies in an area of the Caribbean Sea known for its frequent, devastating hurricanes."

To give your students first-hand experience with persuasive language, propose a fictional controversial situation: A builder wants to purchase a forest area and convince people to build summer "get-away" cottages there. A local conservation group wants the forest maintained as a wildlife preserve. Assign half of the class to create a radio advertisement to convince the reader to buy one of the cottages in the woods and the other half of the class to create a radio advertisement to convince the reader to support the preservation of the natural habitat. Have the students listen to each other's ads and jot down examples of persuasive or connotative language.

Strategies: Reaction Guide; Cooperative Listening

✛ Reaction Guide

A Reaction Guide (Wood, et al., 1992) allows students to react as they listen. This makes the listening task more interactive, resulting in greater comprehension of what's been heard. Explain to your students that authors use words to create visual images and emotional reactions in the reader.

Have the students draw a vertical line in their learning logs, leaving more room on the right side than on the left. As the students listen, have them record striking words, images, or phrases that evoke a response (positive or negative) in the left column. When they have finished listening, ask them to write an explanation for why the words, images, or phrases caused them to react in the column on the right. Model this activity before asking the students to do it independently. For example:

Ideas, words, or phrases that caused a reaction	Because
Indians	I am part Native American, and I do not like my ancestors to be called Indians. They were the first Americans!
wooden huts	The Iroquois lived in domed wooden structures called longhouses. A hut implies something thrown together quickly.

✛ Cooperative Listening

Use this strategy when you give a lecture. Have students listen to your presentation for up to 20 minutes. Then put them into groups of three and hand each group two separate sheets. One sheet has questions about what you presented; the other sheet has the answers. Each answer may be used once or not at all. Each team works together to match the answers to the questions. The students receive a group grade for their effort.

Remember when you prepare this activity, *have more answers than the number of questions (some won't be used) and do not put the answers in the same order as the questions.* For example:

Questions (on one sheet)	Answers (on a different sheet)
1. This gas acts like a blanket in the atmosphere.	a. helium
2. This gas is the most plentiful element in the atmosphere.	b. carbon dioxide
3. This gas is essential for all animal life.	c. argon
	d. oxygen
	e. nitrogen

Answers: 1—b, 2—e, 3—d

Strategies: Possible Sentences; Listening Guide; Listening-Thinking

✛ Possible Sentences

Try this variation of possible sentences (Moore & Moore, 1986):

1. Introduce vocabulary words and put them on the board.
2. Read the passage aloud to the class.
3. As a whole group, call on students and have them state possible sentences using the vocabulary words. Record their statements on the board or the overhead just as the student speaks them, without regard for accuracy.
4. Immediately have the students reread the selection independently.
5. Reread the posted statements.
6. Have students correct any sentences that are wrong.

✛ Listening Guide

A Listening Guide (Castallo, 1976) can help students attend to the important points during a film or other spoken presentation. Here are the steps in this strategy:

1. First, listen to the information yourself, taking notes in the order in which the information is presented.
2. Create a listening guide like the one shown below. Leave blank lines where you want students to fill in the information.
3. Photocopy and distribute the outline.
4. Explain to the students that when they hear the words directly above the lines, the information they need to write on the lines will immediately follow.

Kinds of Precipitation

❋ rain	❋ fog/mist	❋ snow
❋ freezing rain	❋ sleet	❋ hail

✛ Directed Listening-Thinking Activity

Directed Listening-Thinking Activity (Stauffer, 1969) focuses students' concentrations by having them make predictions. Here are the steps:

1. Have students make predictions based on the title and the cover or illustrations. Ask each student to commit to one of the predictions.
2. Read two pages aloud.
3. Ask whether their predictions were accurate.
4. Solicit new predictions and ask each student to commit to one of the new predictions.
5. Read two more pages aloud, then ask how their predictions fared.
6. Continue following this format.

Strategies: Levels of Comprehension

✣ Levels of Comprehension Guide

If at all possible, listen to the presentation ahead of time. In the case of a guest speaker, try to read information prepared by the speaker or talk to the person so you have an idea of what will be said. Prepare a Levels of Comprehension Guide (Vacca and Vacca, 1999) using page 93. Write both true and false statements under each category. Photocopy but do not distribute this to the students. This will prevent them from trying to fill it out during the presentation.

Read aloud the statements and explain that students are going to be listening to a presentation (guest speaker, film, multimedia, etc.) to determine whether the statements were actually made or can be inferred from the information presented. Emphasize that some of the statements are false and not all the answers will be obviously stated. Then have them listen carefully to the presentation. Afterwards, distribute the levels of comprehension guide and give students time to complete the sheet. Collect the papers and go over the answers with the class the next day. During your discussion of the answers, be sure to ask students what clues they used to decide the answer. This will assist struggling students who missed the inferential statements. For this example, students listened to this passage:

A virus is not alive. Yet once it gets into your body, it can take over your living cells and make you sick. The most common viruses are colds and the flu. With most viruses, you will get better within two weeks. However, some viruses—such as AIDS—can eventually kill you. Many deadly viruses are no longer a problem. But this is not due to antibiotics. Antibiotics only fight bacteria. We have vaccines (shots) to keep us from getting viruses. A particular vaccine can only work against a certain virus. That's why you must get separate shots for each virus—such as polio or hepatitis. A vaccine can only protect you from a virus. It cannot fight bacteria because bacteria are living things that change over time.

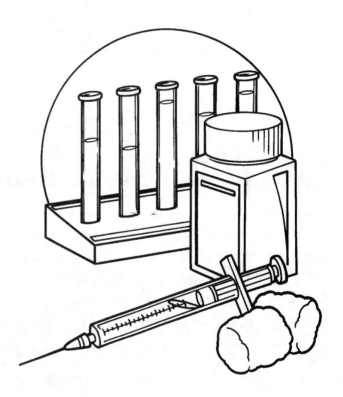

Turn to page 92 for an example of a completed Levels of Comprehension Guide.

Strategies: Levels of Comprehension *(cont.)*

Levels of Comprehension Guide

What was actually said?

Put a checkmark (✓) next to each statement that was made in the information you just listened to.

❏ A virus is a living thing.

☑ Some viruses can kill you.

❏ An antibiotic can help your body to fight a virus.

❏ A single vaccine can work against many viruses.

What does it mean?

Put a checkmark (✓) next to each statement that you feel can be inferred from the material you just heard. Be prepared to explain your choices.

☑ When you have a cold or the flu, you will usually get better within two weeks.

☑ Scientists are looking for a vaccine for AIDS.

❏ Scientists want to create a vaccine for salmonella bacteria.

☑ Polio is a virus.

How can you use this information?

Put a checkmark (✓) next to each statement that you think can be supported from the presentation combined with your background knowledge. Be prepared to defend your response.

❏ When I have a virus, I need to go to the doctor to get an antibiotic.

❏ I need to get a vaccine when I have a virus.

☑ I need to get a vaccine before I ever get a serious virus.

Strategies: Levels of Comprehension *(cont.)*

Graphic Organizer

What was actually said?

Put a checkmark (✓) next to each statement that was made in the information you just listened to.

❑

❑

❑

❑

What does it mean?

Put a checkmark (✓) next to each statement that you feel can be inferred from the material you just heard. Be prepared to explain your choices.

❑

❑

❑

❑

How can you use this information?

Put a checkmark (✓) next to each statement that you think can be supported from the presentation combined with your background knowledge. Be prepared to defend your response.

❑

❑

❑

❑

Strategies: Balancing Bar

✥ Main Idea and Supporting Details: Balancing Bar

Students need to determine the main idea and supporting details while listening. It may help them to envision the main idea as a bar balanced on a top of a column. The column (details) holds up (supports) the main idea. Without the column the bar would fall, just as without details, the main idea is merely a statement without any proof. Using the balancing bar graphic organizer on page 95 is an effective way to represent this. For example:

Redwood trees live longer than any other living thing on Earth. Many have already lived more than 2,000 years because almost nothing can kill them. They do not die from disease, parasites, termites, fungi, or even forest fires. Although its bark may burn, the core of the tree will survive and regrow the bark. When lightning strikes damage them, they will heal. Those blown down by strong winds send up sprouts from the roots that remain in the ground. And if a redwood tree is cut down, its stump will send up saplings.

Main idea: Redwood trees live thousands of years because almost nothing kills them.

Details: They don't die from:

- disease
- parasites
- termites
- fungi
- forest fires
- lightning strikes
- being blown down
- being cut down

Strategies: Balancing Bar *(cont.)*

Graphic Organizer

Main idea:

Details:

Strategies: Weighing the Choices

✤ Weighing the Choices

While they are listening to a debate, students can use the Weighing the Choices Graphic Organizer on page 97.

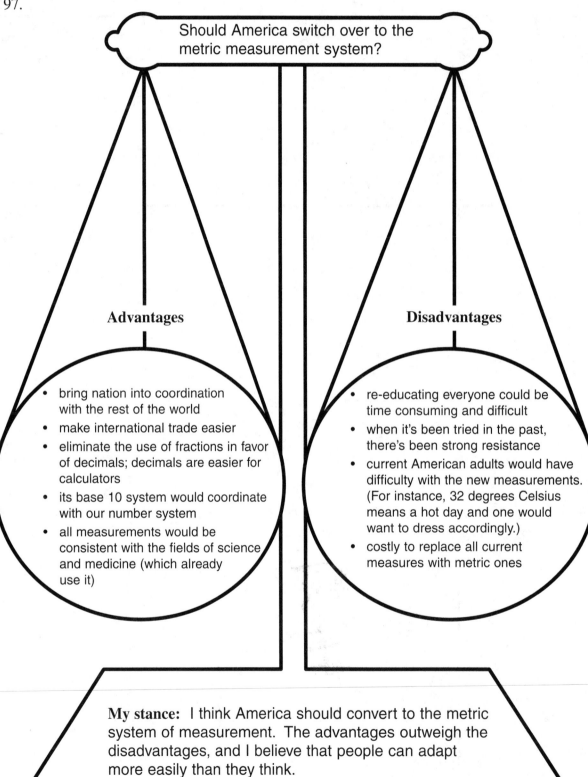

Should America switch over to the metric measurement system?

Advantages

- bring nation into coordination with the rest of the world
- make international trade easier
- eliminate the use of fractions in favor of decimals; decimals are easier for calculators
- its base 10 system would coordinate with our number system
- all measurements would be consistent with the fields of science and medicine (which already use it)

Disadvantages

- re-educating everyone could be time consuming and difficult
- when it's been tried in the past, there's been strong resistance
- current American adults would have difficulty with the new measurements. (For instance, 32 degrees Celsius means a hot day and one would want to dress accordingly.)
- costly to replace all current measures with metric ones

My stance: I think America should convert to the metric system of measurement. The advantages outweigh the disadvantages, and I believe that people can adapt more easily than they think.

Strategies: Weighing the Choices *(cont.)*

Graphic Organizer

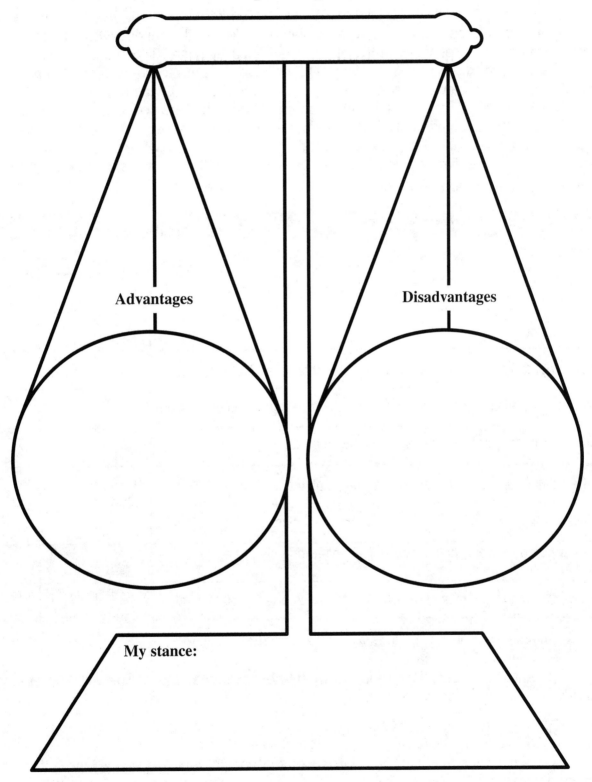

Advantages

Disadvantages

My stance:

Strategies: Considering the Source

✢ Considering the Source

Students can use the checklist on page 99 to determine the credibility of an oral account. An example:

A couple visited a museum and saw a display of stuffed rattlesnakes with a placard stating that most rattlesnakes in the region live in nearby Mine Kill State Park. The next day they went to that park to see Mine Kill Falls. On the path to the falls, the woman stopped when she saw a snake lying on a rock. She thought it was a rattlesnake because it looked like the ones in the museum. The snake was coiled up, so no one could see if it had rattles on its tail. The man said that even though the coloring was right, it did not have the flattened head of a rattlesnake. He convinced the woman to walk past it. She believes it was a rattler. He disagrees. Whom should you believe?

Circle the symbol under the correct column.

Ask yourself	Yes	No	Unsure
Did the person actually see what happened or live through the event?	👍	👎	?
Has anyone else claimed to have seen what happened or lived through the same event?	👍	👎	?
Was the account of the other person(s) similar?	👍	👎	?
Does the person have any evidence (photo, videotape, audio tape, etc.)?	👍	👎	?
Could fear, excitement, or poor viewing conditions have influenced the person?	👍	👎	?
Could other people or their claims have influenced the person?	👍	👎	?
Did the person report what happened immediately after it happened?	👍	👎	?
Was the person awake, aware, and not under the influence of drugs?	👍	👎	?
Does the person have a reputation for honesty among his or her coworkers and acquaintances?	👍	👎	?
Is the person apt to get money or publicity (fame) as a result of this claim?	👍	👎	?

The more "thumbs up" you circled, the stronger the case for believing.
Reasons for Believing: I circled ___4___ 👍 .
They both saw the snake. She reported what she saw immediately. She will not get any money or fame from her claim.

The more "thumbs down" you circled, the stronger the case for disbelieving.
Reasons for Disbelieving: I circled ___3___ 👎 .
The museum display or fear may have influenced the woman. She has no evidence. If she had taken a photo, she could have compared it to the ones at the museum or a picture in a book.

If you circled four or more question marks (**?**), you need more information before you can decide to believe.
Because I circled three **?** and three 👎, I am doubtful it was a rattlesnake.

Strategies: Considering the Source *(cont.)*

Graphic Organizer

Circle the symbol under the correct column.

Ask yourself	Yes	No	Unsure
Did the person actually see what happened or live through the event?	👍	👎	?
Has anyone else claimed to have seen what happened or lived through the same event?	👍	👎	?
Was the account of the other person(s) similar?	👍	👎	?
Does the person have any evidence (photo, videotape, audio tape, etc.)?	👍	👎	?
Could fear, excitement, or poor viewing conditions have influenced the person?	👎	👍	?
Could other people have influenced the person?	👎	👍	?
Did the person report what happened immediately after it happened?	👍	👎	?
Was the person awake, aware, and not under the influence of drugs?	👍	👎	?
Does the person have a reputation for honesty among his or her co-workers and acquaintances?	👍	👎	?
Is the person apt to get money or publicity (fame) as a result of this claim?	👎	👍	?

The more "thumbs up" you circled, the stronger the case for believing.

Reasons for Believing: I circled _____ 👍 .

_____

The more "thumbs down" you circled, the stronger the case for disbelieving.

Reasons for Disbelieving: I circled _____ 👎 .

_____

If you circled four or more question marks (**?**), you need more information before you can decide whether or not to believe.

Strategies: Collaborative Listening

✢ Collaborative Listening/Viewing Guide

The Collaborative Listening/Viewing Guide (Wood, et al 1992) has four steps:

1. Give a preview of an upcoming presentation (such as a slide presentation, videotape, DVD, television show, or guest speaker) while your students listen without taking any notes.

2. Students should note key words and important ideas that they hear during the presentation.

3. Have students get together with partners immediately or as soon as possible after the presentation and use what they heard to create a mind map or to answer questions you pose.

4. Synthesize by having the whole class reconvene to discuss and, if necessary, add to their mind maps or answers.

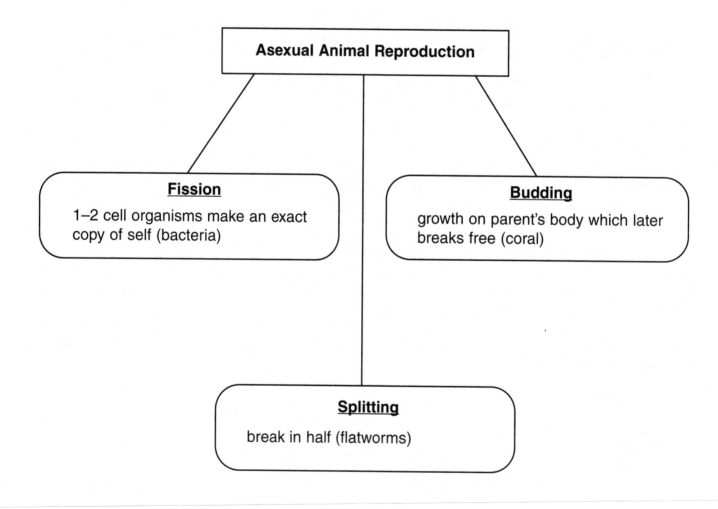

Introduction to Section 5: Remembering Nonfiction

Much of education relies upon memory. In today's educational environment, once a standard or benchmark is met at one level, the students are expected to have permanently gained that knowledge; it is not necessarily covered again. Students are expected to build upon that knowledge—which means that they had better remember it.

Memory is not a "one strategy fits all" cognitive function. What works to bolster one person's memory will not necessarily help another. This section outlines many ways that you can improve your students' ability to recall expository information. It begins with some quick and easy ideas and moves on to more elaborate methods. All of them have research-based proof that they increase memory. Try as many of them as you can possibly squeeze into your curriculum.

Strategies: Songs; Quick Review; Acronyms; Mind Maps

✛ Songs and Rhymes

Singing information is a powerful way to store information in permanent memory. A stunning example of the power of song came from an informal study of college students who had learned the 50 states and their capitals. After five years the only students who had retained all of the information were those who had been taught to sing the states and their capitals.

Rhymes are powerful memory boosters, too. For example, many of us rely on the ancient rhyme, "Thirty Days Hath September" to determine how many days are in a particular month.

✛ Quick Review

At the start of a lesson, spend five minutes recalling (as partners) and recording at least three highlights from the prior day's lesson. This is especially effective if you pair a capable student with a struggling student or an English as a second language learner.

✛ Acronyms

Acronyms help students memorize. You may recognize Roy G. Biv as a common acronym for remembering the colors of the rainbow in order (red, orange, yellow, green, blue, indigo, and violet). Researchers have found individually created acronyms the most effective. The mental stimulation needed to think of an acronym puts the information into long-term memory.

✛ Independent Mind Maps

Self-created mind maps provide a vehicle to move concepts into long-term memory. One of the best ways to show students how to create their own mind maps is by demonstrating your own metacognitive processing and the resulting mind map through a think-aloud on at least three separate occasions. It is important that the students individually create mind maps. Research has shown that students can most easily recall information stored in a personalized mind map because they can readily visualize it.

Strategies: You Are There; Five Fingers; Internalized Response

✣ You Are There

This strategy (Wood, et al., 1992) increases understanding and retention of material by having the student put him/herself into another person's shoes. Assign the students a role and ask them questions about the topic. They need to speak in character to answer the questions. Students usually find this challenging but engaging.

Here are some examples of a few of the roles your students could assume:

- ✦ demonstrators in favor of (or opposed to) women's suffrage
- ✦ colonists who were loyal to the king during the Revolutionary War
- ✦ former slaves (or former masters) in the Deep South during Reconstruction
- ✦ people in favor of (or opposed to) the Vietnam War

✣ Five Fingers

This strategy works when students need to remember data sets with five elements. They can use their "built-in" organizer— five fingers to remember the information. Have students assign a piece of data to each finger on one hand. This only works if you have data set of five because the student needs to know that there is one for each finger on one hand. The illustration to the right is an example:

✣ Internalized Response

Internalized response creates long-lasting memories by having students relate the ideas in a passage to their own experiences. Have the students draw two columns in a learning log and label them with the headings: "What the Passage Said" and "My Response."

What the Passage Said	My Response
Iguanas cannot be trained.	I'm glad that I have a dog. He can do tricks, and that's cool.
Male sea horses give birth to live babies.	That's weird! Females are always the ones having babies.

Strategies: Life Experiences; Highlighting; Key Words

❖ Life Experiences Vocabulary

Students retain vocabulary knowledge when they associate the new words with experiences. They can do this by generating a sentence for each new word. Use this technique in whole-class discussions, so that in case a student can't think of a personal example, they can adopt someone else's. Have students record the words down the left side of a learning log and the life-experience sentences on the right.

Vocabulary Word to Remember	Sentence About My Life Experience
exacerbate	If Mom sprays water on a chemical fire in the kitchen, it will only exacerbate the problem.
ludicrous	My friend Janna looked ludicrous when she came to the door on a hot July day wearing her new winter coat.

❖ Judicious Highlighting

Have you ever opened a used college textbook and been overwhelmed by the amount of highlighted text that assaulted your eyes? Too many students highlight almost everything, essentially rendering the technique useless. Teach proper highlighting and text annotating by projecting a transparency of a textbook page and marking it as the students follow along on a photocopy. You can also provide time at the end of class or the start of the next class for students to review the notes they've written to highlight essential information or add additional details.

❖ Key Word Imaging

Key word imaging (Blachowicz & Ogle, 2001) helps students to recall categories of information. If your class needs to remember four different types of clouds, encourage your students to think of clever mental images that will help them to recall the types of cloud formations, such as:

cirrus clouds—clouds that look like they've been cut to shreds by scissors

stratus—thin flat gray sheets (overcast) that straddle the sky

cumulus—clouds that look like clumps of whipped cream or cotton balls

cumulonimbus—ominous thunderheads that reach high into the sky

Note that the images may include mnemonic cues, too. Key word imaging works best if the class generates its own key word images, so resist the urge to tell them what to imagine.

Strategies: Summarizing; A-B-C Summary; SQ3R

✤ Summarizing

An excellent technique for long-term remembering lies in having students put new information into their own words. Read aloud a few pages of *The Important Book* by Margaret Wise Brown (HarperCollins, 1999). Have students use the book's format to write a summary about a topic you've studied:

> But the important thing about a variable is that it always stands for a number in an equation. Sometimes a variable is called the unknown.
> You use a letter—often an *x*, *y*, or *n*—as a variable.

✤ A-B-C Summary

An A-B-C summary increases retention because students process information thoroughly. Pair the students. Give a term and ask them to think of a word, phrase, or sentence for each letter. Allow "ex" words for the letter X. Have each pair submit their A-B-C summary to you. For example:

F ourths are ¼, ²⁄₄, ¾, and ⁴⁄₄
R atio of two numbers
A dd them only if you have common denominators
C ommon factors can go into the numerator and denominator
T op and bottom numbers identical means one whole (example, ⅝)
I mproper fractions have larger number on the top
O n the bottom is the denominator
N umerator is the number on top
S how part of a whole

✤ SQ3R

SQ3R (Robinson, 1961) is the grandparent of all study strategies. Robinson believed the method had to become automatic, so that the learner did the steps without having to think about them. Therefore, if you use this method, do it often enough to make it second nature for your students. Here are the steps:

S ➔ **Survey** the chapter: Preview the objectives, headings, margin notes, graphs, photos, and illustrations.

Q ➔ **Question** yourself: "What do I already know about this subject? What do I need to know about it?" Then turn the side headings into questions.

➔ **Read:** To answer the questions.

3R ➔ **Recite:** Orally summarize what you just read. This step is crucial to solidify it in your memory.

➔ **Review:** Go back through the material, this time taking notes on the key points. Follow up with brief reviews of the material on a frequent basis to achieve the best long-term retention.

Strategies: Circle of Knowledge; Question Exchange

✛ Circle of Knowledge Review

The circle of knowledge lets students review lots of material in a short period of time.

1. Give every student an index card. Each student writes one question on the front and another on the back. These are questions that he or she can correctly answer about the nonfiction unit. You should do a card, too, writing two questions that you don't think the students will ask.

2. Form a circle with you included. Have the students call out 1-2-1-2 (like in gym class).

3. Have all of the number ones step forward two steps and turn around to face the number twos. They ask the number twos the two questions they have prepared and tell the correct answer if the respondent gets it wrong. Then the number two students ask their two questions of the number ones. Now both students in each set should know the correct answer to four questions.

4. Monitor this activity closely to decide when to call out, "Switch cards and take one step to the right!" The number ones switch cards with the number twos, then take a step to the right and repeat the questioning. Continue with this activity until the students have come full circle or you run out of time.

✛ Question Exchange

A question exchange lets students review information using their own questions. Each student prepares five thought-provoking questions and answers for homework; these questions cannot have yes or no answers. Each student then poses one of these questions to a classmate in round-robin fashion. The classmate gives an answer, then asks a question of the next student. It's best if students ask one of their questions that has not already been asked; however, if necessary, they may repeat one. This strategy is excellent for review because each student ends up knowing the answers to his or her original five questions plus the answers to all of those questions presented in class. Here is how it works:

Alicia: (*To Benito*) "What territories did the USA acquire as a result of the Spanish American War?"

Benito: "Puerto Rico, the Philippines, and Guam."

Alicia: "Right."

Benito: (*To Christa*) "When did the Spanish-American War begin and when did it end?"

Christa: "1861 to 1865."

Benito: "Sorry, that's wrong."

Benito: (*To Dylan*) "When did the Spanish-American War begin and when did it end?"

Dylan: "The Spanish-American war started and ended in 1898."

Strategies: Scattergories

✛ Scattergories

Playing this game will help students remember information and enjoy themselves at the same time! Choose a topic and letters that spell a four-letter word (it does not have to relate to the subject). It helps if the word has some of the most commonly used letters in it: R, A, L, N, E, S, and T. Students put a term or phrase in each box. They earn 2 points for a valid, unique response no one else in the class has; 1 point for a valid response some else has; and no points if they did not have a valid response. If challenged by a classmate, students must explain how their responses relate to the subject. Before photocopying page 107, write the word you chose and the categories across the top. In the fourth column, you can write "People." When you use only three categories, use the fourth column for recording points.

World War I

	Vocabulary/Phrases	Events	Places	
C	Central Powers	colonies taken from Germany after war		
A	armistice	assassination of Austria Archduke	Austria-Hungary	
P	poison gas used in battle	Paris Peace Conference	Portugal	
S	Schlieffen plan	strategy for battles	Serbia	

Strategies: Scattergories *(cont.)*

Graphic Organizers

	Vocabulary/Phrases	Events	Places	

	Vocabulary/Phrases	Events	Places	

Strategies: Home-School Folder

✤ Home-School Folder

Create for each student a home-school folder that contains student work. Send them home each week on Friday, ask for a parent signature, and have students return them on Mondays. Use the form given on page 109. On Fridays the students fill in the form, giving them an opportunity to review and synthesize what's been learned that week. It also provides an opening for discussion with parents about school. When the folders are returned, keep the forms in each student's folder or a portfolio as a record of learning throughout the year. In middle school, this could be a grade-level initiative with the homeroom teachers taking responsibility for distributing and collecting the folders each week.

Dear Parent,   Week of _____

This is a summary of my week.
Please read it, write a comment, and sign it. I must return it on Monday.

In **math**, I did word problems and had a quiz on inequalities.	In **science**, I learned the properties of 20 different minerals.
In **social studies**, We discussed events leading up to the Civil War and studied the abolitionists Frederick Douglass and William Lloyd Garrison.	In **language arts**, I practiced listening to nonfiction passages and writing a summary of what we had heard. I also did research for my inquiry project on castles.
This is how I did: ___V___ Following directions ___I___ Listening ___G___ Keeping my stuff neat ___G___ Participating in class **V = Very good** **G = Good** **I = I need to improve**	**Parent comments and signature:** You really covered a lot in just one week. I'm proud of you! ____*Tina Yang*_____ *(parent signature)*

Strategies: Home-School Folder *(cont.)*

Graphic Organizer

Dear Parent,   Week of _____

This is a summary of my week.
Please read it, write a comment, and sign it. I must return it on Monday.

In **math**,	In **science**,

In **social studies**,	In **language arts**,

This is how I did:

_____ Following directions
_____ Listening
_____ Keeping my stuff neat
_____ Participating in class

V = Very good
G = Good
I = I need to improve

Parent comments and signature:

_____
(parent signature)

Strategies: Bare Bones Summary

✣ Bare Bones Summary

A bare bones summary works well with a short expository passage. If you use it with a longer passage, provide students with additional copies of the graphic organizer on page 111. Have students read the passage and then identify the minimum number of words that will carry the message. They record the words or phrases in order, resulting in the "bare bones" of the information. When studying the graphic organizer, the students strengthen their memories by having to "flesh out" the details.

Albert Einstein

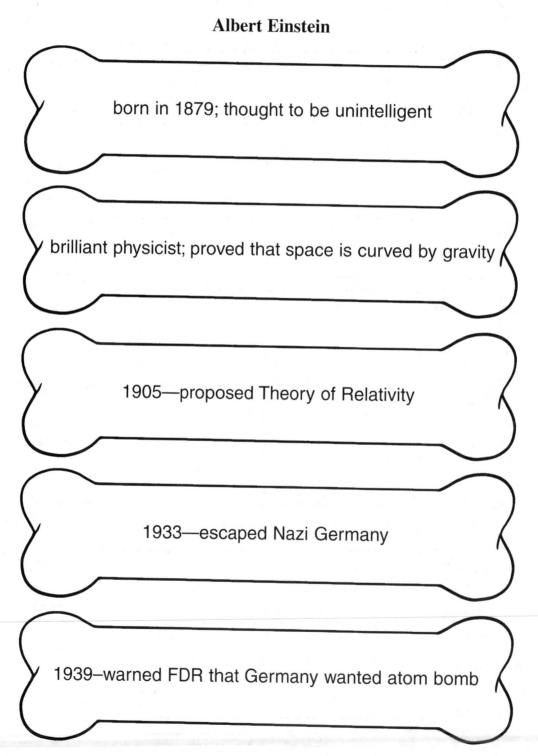

born in 1879; thought to be unintelligent

brilliant physicist; proved that space is curved by gravity

1905—proposed Theory of Relativity

1933—escaped Nazi Germany

1939–warned FDR that Germany wanted atom bomb

Strategies: Bare Bones Summary *(cont.)*

Graphic Organizer

Strategies: Informal Notes Outline

⁑ Informal Notes Outline

Outlines are essentially the main ideas and important details from a text. Teach your students how to create outlines by providing three-stage scaffolding. For example:

> People have damaged the Amazon rain forest. They have removed soil in search of precious metals. Dams built for water power have backed up rivers, drowning everything for more than 1,000 miles. Millions of trees are cut down every year for furniture. Dozens of types of plants and animals become extinct daily.

Here's how the outline would look for this paragraph for each of the different stages:

Stage 1: You provide all of the details; students must identify the main idea.

Main Idea: _____

D1: _____People have removed soil._____

D2: _____Dams built for water power have drowned many living things._____

D3: _____Millions of trees are cut down every year._____

D4: _____Dozens of types of plants and animals become extinct daily._____

Stage 2: You give the main idea and two details; the students must provide the other details.

Main Idea: _People have damaged the Amazon rain forest._____

D1: _____People have removed soil._____

D2: _____

D3: _____Millions of trees are cut down every year._____

D4: _____

Stage 3: You provide only one detail; students must supply the main idea and all other details.

Main Idea: _____

D1: _____

D2: _____

D3: _____

D4: _____Dozens of types of plants and animals become extinct daily._____

After the students have had enough practice with this strategy to become competent at generating outlines, you can have them prepare their own informal outlines as they read nonfiction text.

Strategies: Informal Notes Outline *(cont.)*

Graphic Organizer

Main Idea: _____

    D1: _____

    D2: _____

    D3: _____

    D4: _____

Main Idea: _____

    D1: _____

    D2: _____

    D3: _____

    D4: _____

Main Idea: _____

    D1: _____

    D2: _____

    D3: _____

    D4: _____

Main Idea: _____

    D1: _____

    D2: _____

    D3: _____

    D4: _____

Strategies: Key Word Notes

✥ Key Word Notes

Key word notes is a method that lets students develop effective notes while reading or listening to class lectures. Introduce the skill by recording the key words derived from a chapter's headings down the left edge of the paper. Depending upon the needs of your students, you may also want to include the page number on which the key word appears. Leave four or five blank lines (or more if appropriate) after each key word. Draw a vertical line to separate the key word from the note section, leaving lots more space on the right-hand side. Photocopy and distribute. Have the students review the key words prior to reading or listening. This sets a purpose: to find and record in their own words an expanded version of the key words. After they have used this strategy twice and demonstrated competence, students can generate their own key words from the section headings.

Chapter 16: Pollution

pollution is (page 41)

Pollution is damage done to the Earth created by waste. Pollution can hurt plants, animals, and humans.

pollution affects (page 42)

Pollution affects land, air, or water.

types of pollution (pp. 41–43)

There are many types of pollution:

- solid waste (trash, litter, junk)
- air pollution (gases, smoke, chemicals, acid rain)
- land pollution (chemicals, nuclear waste, solid waste)
- water pollution (heat, chemicals, solid waste)
- noise pollution (loud sounds)

global warming (page 44)

Global warming is a theory that proposes that the Earth is warming up due to excessive carbon dioxide in the atmosphere. The carbon dioxide comes from the cars, homes, and factories that burn gas, oil, and coal.

To study, have students lay out their notes in overlapping pages so that only the key words show and try to recite the information in the explanation column.

Students who choose key word notes for research can go through their notes and highlight in different colors the key words for each topic. This makes it easy to collect the information that belongs together. For example, if a student is doing a report on a place, he or she can highlight all the key words for information about physical characteristics in yellow, climate in blue, types of life found there in pink, surprising or unique characteristics in green, etc.

Strategies: Text Response Centers

⁑ Text Response Centers

Text response centers (Keene & Zimmerman, 1997) create lasting impressions while enabling your students to use their multiple intelligences. Rotate your students through these centers:

- ◈ **Drama**—At the drama center a group of students can act out the events they have read about. They can write a script, assign and memorize parts, and perform it for the class. They can also develop a Readers Theater script or do pantomime.

- ◈ **Models**—At this center students can create models of their strongest images from the text. Provide chenille sticks (pipe cleaners), plenty of tagboard, oaktag, or sturdy cardboard, modeling clay in many colors, tape, glue stick, scissors, cotton balls, and craft sticks.

- ◈ **Writer's Nook**—At the writer's nook the student describes a personal reaction to the text. The writer's nook needs lined paper, stapler and staples, pencils or pens of different colors, construction paper, glue, and scissors. Students can create a construction paper or oaktag frame around their written work and hang it up for others to read in the room or hall. They can also tape a lined sheet of paper to the bottom of the frame. This paper will allow readers to react to what the writer said.

- ◈ **Studio**—In the studio each student creates an artistic response to text. The studio needs different sizes of unlined paper, colored pencils, markers, glue stick, fabric scraps, string, scissors, watercolor paints, and brushes. The students can choose to exhibit their artwork in the room or hall. They can also tape a lined sheet of paper to the bottom of the frame to allow viewers to write their reactions to the artist's creation. Occasionally ask students to explain their work to the class, telling why they selected the media and colors they used to express their ideas.

Randomly highlight student work from each center. This lets the students know that you value what they have produced and gives you an opportunity to demonstrate to the rest of the class the kinds of things you want to see produced at each center. For example, you can read aloud a student's response from the writer's nook and say, "I liked how John used red ink to write his response to the passage we read about the Native American treaties being repeatedly broken. It helps to show me that he understood the tribes' anger at not being able to rely on the government's promises."

Strategies: Roundtable Alphabet

⁘ Roundtable Alphabet

The Roundtable Alphabet (Ricci & Wahlgren, 1998) is a useful tool for review of material. The completed chart serves as a memory prompt for terms, facts, or events related to the topic.

1. Assign students to teams of three.

2. Give each team one blank copy of the Roundtable Alphabet on page 117.

3. Ask students to come up with a word or phrase that begins with each letter of the alphabet. Allow students to use words that begin with the letters "ex" for the X space. Each team tries to fill in as many boxes as possible within a specified time period. Do not take off points for any spaces the team didn't fill in, unless it is obvious that they aren't even trying.

4. Have the teams write a definition for each term/phrase on the reverse side of the paper.

5. Create a classroom compilation alphabet, photocopy it, and distribute it to class members as a study aid.

Directions: Write a word or a phrase that relates to the topic and begins with each letter.

Topic: Math Terms	A acute angle	B base	C circum-ference	D distributive property	E equation	F fraction
G graphs	H height	I integer	J	K kilometer	L less than	M mean
N negative numbers	O order of operations	P perimeter	Q quotient	R reciprocal	S symmetry	T trapezoid
U unit of	V variable	W whole number	X exponent	Y y-axis	Z zero	

Strategies: Roundtable Alphabet *(cont.)*

Directions: Write a word or a phrase that relates to the topic and begins with each letter.

Topic:	A	B	C	D	E	F
G	H	I	J	K	L	M
N	O	P	Q	R	S	T
U	V	W	X	Y	Z	

Strategies: Knowledge Tier

❖ Knowledge Tier

A knowledge tier encourages students to concentrate on memorizing the most crucial elements of a topic. Prior to beginning a nonfiction unit, design a knowledge tier, using page 119. For the base tier, choose the three to five most important concepts that the students should remember and build on throughout their lives. This is core knowledge that all literate adults know. For the middle tier, choose the three to five concepts that will be useful knowledge—things that may be forgotten after the unit but that the student may be able to recall years later in response to a stimulus. At the top put the three to five details that will definitely be forgotten after the unit is over. These things most literate adults do not know (although they would probably know how to locate the information). Display the knowledge tier and guide your class to ask questions about the items you've put in the bottom two tiers.

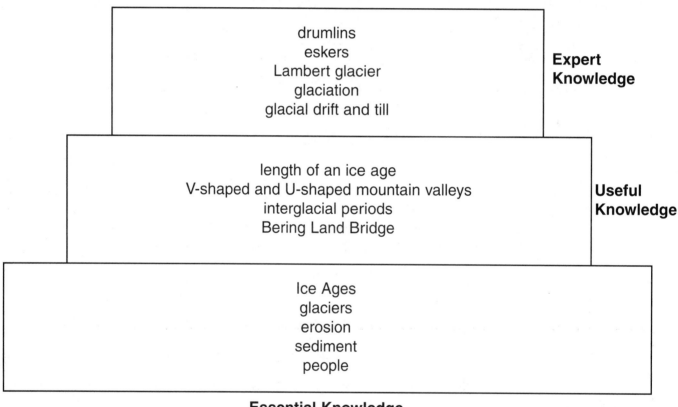

Expert Knowledge

drumlins
eskers
Lambert glacier
glaciation
glacial drift and till

Useful Knowledge

length of an ice age
V-shaped and U-shaped mountain valleys
interglacial periods
Bering Land Bridge

Ice Ages
glaciers
erosion
sediment
people

Essential Knowledge

Class-generated questions:

- ✦ What are Ice Ages?
- ✦ What are glaciers?
- ✦ What is erosion?
- ✦ What is sediment?
- ✦ Did people live through the Ice Ages? How did they survive?

- ✦ How long does an ice age last?
- ✦ What does the shape of mountain valleys have to do with this topic?
- ✦ What are interglacial periods? When did they happen?
- ✦ What is the Bering Land Bridge? Where is it?

Strategies: Knowledge Tier *(cont.)*

Graphic Organizer

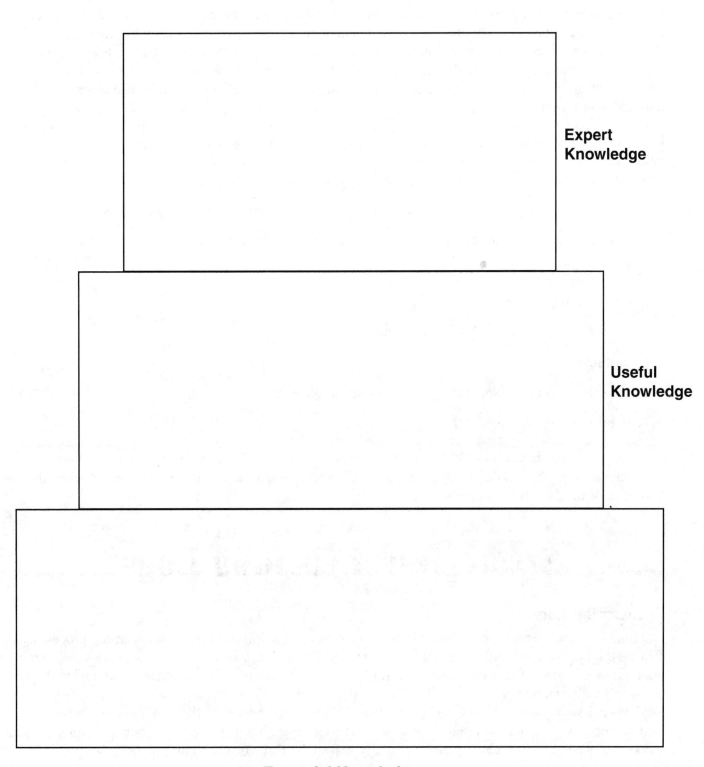

**Expert
Knowledge**

**Useful
Knowledge**

Essential Knowledge

Introduction to Section 6: Writing Nonfiction

Writing is one of the most difficult skills to teach because it is such a multifaceted, complex task, encompassing a broad range of abilities. Students may be asked to compose a response to a presentation they heard or devise a summary of a text that they have read. They may be told to draw conclusions or take a stance and defend it. And whenever they write, they must consider the audience, decide what to include, choose appropriate words, and sequence the material in a logical order. That's a tall order for anyone!

Fortunately, no one has to write something perfectly on the first try, and students need to know that published authors—even the most famous ones—spend many hours rewriting, revising, and reorganizing. The steps in this writing process are as follows:

1. brainstorming/idea gathering (for ideas see Preparing Students for Nonfiction section)

2. categorizing and clustering ideas (for ideas see Preparing Students for Nonfiction section)

3. writing a first draft

4. conferencing with a teacher or peer

5. revising for clarity, possibly reorganizing

6. writing a second draft

7. revising for accurate spelling, grammar, punctuation, etc.

8. publishing and sharing the final copy with others

All formal writing should follow the steps of the writing process. However, with informal writing (such as learning logs or graphic organizers), merely getting the ideas down without regard for spelling, grammar, or mechanics is more desirable.

Strategies: Learning Logs

✛ Learning Logs

Learning logs are a time-efficient way for students to become involved in their own learning process by sharing their ideas and questions in a safe environment. A student who rarely speaks in class may write volumes in a journal. Some educators have students summarize what they have learned and what they still don't understand after each lesson. Others tell students to ask questions they'd like answered. Students can write their questions and record the answers as they discover them in a journal, submitting it to you only when a question remains unanswered after several days of the unit. Journal writing works best when done for about 10 minutes daily, especially if the teacher participates by writing in a journal, too.

Strategies: Formulating Leads; Active Verbs

✢ Formulating Leads and Conclusions

Students should model their writing after real-world sources such as magazines, Web pages, personal interviews, videos, etc. William Zinsser, a well-respected editor and nonfiction author, emphasizes that the first sentence (lead) is the most important in any nonfiction piece. The lead must pull readers in, compelling them to read the entire article, book, etc. Expose your students to a variety of leads and encourage them to use them in their own writing. It will result in a pleasant improvement in the quality of their written compositions. Well-written lead sentences:

- ✦ show instead of tell (vivid imagery)
- ✦ raise a question or issue that the article attempts to answer (Example: "Should grizzly bears be protected from hunters?")
- ✦ surprise or shock the reader
- ✦ open with a climax, then go into a flashback of events leading up to that climax—effective for historical events

The conclusion is almost as important as the lead. Teach students to consciously determine when they are finished by asking themselves these pertinent questions:

- ✦ Did I include all the essential information?
- ✦ Did I leave any "loose ends"?
- ✦ Did I answer all the questions I raised (if any)?
- ✦ Will the reader be satisfied if I end here?

✢ Using Active Verbs

Students write better when they reduce the use of passive voice (any form of the verb "to be"). Information is best conveyed through the use of nouns, active verbs, and a minimum of adjectives and adverbs. Encourage sound writing practices with the following exercise:

1. Choose a topic that is familiar to your students (in this example, the forest).
2. Have the class brainstorm a list of related nouns.
3. Have the class brainstorm a list of actions (verbs) that each noun could do.
4. Ask the students to write a paragraph using the nouns and verbs.

Nouns (people, places, things, ideas)	Verbs (what each noun can do)
tree	stands, sways
sunlight	shines, gleams, glows, hides
bees	buzz, hum, fly
birds	fly, sing, twitter
branches	bend, sway, break
rabbit	hops, runs, eats, twitches nose

Here's a student's composition based on the words generated in the brainstormed list:

On this warm summer day sunlight gleams through the leaves of the forest. The air is filled with the sound of bees buzzing and birds twittering as they fly from one branch to another. A movement on the forest floor catches Ricardo's eye. He turns in time to see a flash of a white cottontail as a rabbit hops away.

Strategies: Editing Conferences; Peer Editing; Praise-Question-Polish

✛ Editing Conferences

At editing conferences your goal is to help the students to assess their own work. This means you should ask questions more often than you give suggestions. Here are some good questions to ask to make students reflect on the quality of their own work:

1. What is the most important point? Why?

2. Do you see anything that doesn't fit?

3. Read aloud your best description. What makes this section the best?

4. Are there any places where you could have gone into more detail?

5. After reading this, I have these questions: _____, _____, and _____. Do you think that you could answer them in your paper?

✛ Peer Editing

For peer editing conferences, establish small, heterogeneous groups. The first student writer reads his or her piece and asks for specific feedback, such as "Have I explained _____ clearly enough?" or "Is this an effective lead?" or "Can you think of a better way to say _____?" Others in the group give their suggestions for improvement. Then the next student writer presents his or her piece. They continue in this manner until all group members have had an opportunity to have their pieces critiqued.

✛ Praise-Question-Polish

An excellent technique for teaching peer editing is Praise-Question-Polish (Lyons, 1981). Prominently post the steps of the strategy. After students have written a first draft, they meet with a partner. The first student reads his or her paper to the other, and then asks:

Praise: "What do you like best?"

Question: "What questions do you have?"

Polish: "What kinds of additions, or corrections are needed? Do I need to reorganize?"

These questions are repeated after the second partner reads his or her work aloud.

Strategies: Past Events; Experience Writing

❖ Writing About a Past Event

Ask your students to write as much as they can recall about their most recent birthday. The students may be amazed at how much they have forgotten about what happened. Ask them how they could go about finding out more (referring to photographs or a home videotape; asking parents, siblings, and friends) in order to reconstruct that date. After conducting their investigation, have them incorporate the extra information they gleaned from these sources to create a brief essay. This activity demonstrates how historians must use a variety of resources to help them determine what truly happened in the past.

❖ Experience Writing

Experience writing is a series of steps that guides students in putting together a composition about a personally experienced event. You need to think about the needs of your class when determining how many sessions this will take.

1. Take a field trip. The students should engage in the steps that a nonfiction author takes in preparing expository text: taking notes on the trip and asking questions.
2. As a whole group, brainstorm all that you recall from the trip. Record the information on the board.
3. As a whole group ask the students to categorize the information into three groups.
4. Using an overhead, guide the students in using as many words in each group as possible to compose three paragraphs (one for each category). Write each paragraph on a separate transparency.
5. Have the class suggest different sequences for the paragraphs on the overhead. This is simplified by overlapping the individual transparencies and rearranging them. After each organization, have the class chorally read the piece from start to finish.
6. Have the class vote determine the order of the paragraphs.
7. Ask for suggested lead sentences. Record these on another transparency. Read them aloud to the class and have the class vote on the best lead.
8. Ask for suggested concluding sentences. Record these on another transparency. Read them aloud to the class and have the class vote on the best conclusion.
9. Type or handwrite a final version with the paragraph organization, lead, and closing sentences the students selected. Photocopy it and hand it out to each class member.
10. Have the students copy it into their journals or onto another paper.

The next time you take a field trip, have your students independently design a nonfiction account of their experience. This method lets the students "discover" the questions every nonfiction writer asks himself or herself prior to writing a piece:

- ✦ Who is my audience?
- ✦ What do my readers need to know?
- ✦ Do I want to include this piece of information? Why or why not?
- ✦ In what order should I present the information?
- ✦ How should I present the material (organization, voice, etc.)?
- ✦ What visuals do I need?

As students expand their awareness of the many ingredients that go into the creation of an expository piece, they will not only improve their ability to write nonfiction pieces but also grow in their understanding of how to find information.

Strategies: Writing in Response to Text

✣ Writing in Response to Text

There are many ways for students to respond to expository text. Here is a list of some responses that you could ask your students to compose. Each suggestion is followed by an example.

✦ a play featuring several famous people from history (*Queen Isabella and Christopher Columbus*)

✦ a diary or log (*a captain's log of the Mayflower voyage*)

✦ advertisements (*extol the amazing characteristics of the Egyptian pyramids*)

✦ a manual (*how to care for a panda bear*)

✦ frequently-asked questions and answers about a topic (*FAQ about AIDS*)

✦ songs or poems—with lyrics that rhyme or not (*poem about the Civil War*)

✦ brochures or travel guides (*interesting places to visit in Alabama*)

✦ a Web page (*how to treat plantar's warts*)

✦ catalog page (*descriptions, illustrations, and realistic prices for art supplies*)

✦ alphabet books about a subject (*music*)

✦ Powerpoint presentation (*adobe dwellings*)

✦ diorama accompanied by labels or a brief description of the scene (*an Iroquois longhouse*)

✦ poster or bulletin board (*the oxygen cycle*)

✦ picture book for younger students (*life in a coral reef*)

✦ photo essay (*kinds of railroad cars*)

✦ scrapbook (*past Super Bowls*)

✦ script of a newscast for a major world event (*Pearl Harbor attack*)

✦ two major historical figures exchange fact-filled letters (*George Washington and King George*)

✦ write and perform a "karaoke" version of a videotape with the sound muted (*John F. Kennedy's assassination*)

✦ Have students develop a list of questions they would ask during an interview with a famous person, either from today or the past. (*What would you like to ask Napoleon?*)

✦ Write a dialogue that might have occurred between two people in history such as military leaders, government leaders, or scientists. (*the talk that took place between Ulysses Grant and Robert E. Lee in the Appomattox Court House*)

✦ Have students assume the persona of an inanimate object involved in an historic event and write about it from the inanimate object's viewpoint. (*the theater box or a seat next to Lincoln at his assassination*)

✦ Ask students to work in groups to create a rap song, rhymed verse, or couplets that summarize key ideas from an expository passage.

Strategies: RAFT

✦ Creative Nonfiction Writing Using RAFT

RAFT (Santa, 1988) stands for Role, Audience, Form, and Topic. This method challenges students to prepare an unusual, creative response by actively processing information rather than just regurgitating it. Always clarify your expectations by reading aloud an example prior to assigning students a specific RAFT project. Post these questions for students to consider before they begin writing:

◆ What would my viewpoint be as _____?
◆ Why would I be writing to _____?
◆ What would I want or need to say to my audience?

Your Role as Writer	Audience for Piece	Form of Writing	Topic
travel agent	tourists	pamphlet	reasons to visit Wyoming
sailor	self	diary	dangers of life on the sea
funeral director	newspaper readers	obituary	life and accomplishments of Theodore Roosevelt
pharmacist	public	instructions	dangers of mixing drugs and alcohol
attorney	U.S. Supreme Court	appeal speech	*Brown vs. Board of Education*
figurative language	middle school students	job description	use in compositions
radio news reporter	listening audience	script	start of Cuban Missile crisis
talk show host	television viewers	talk show script	discussion of stem cell research
constituent	U.S. Senator or Representative	petition	need for legislation to protect endangered wildlife
newswriter	public	newspaper article	Johnstown Flood of 1889
Winston Churchill	Ann Landers	advice column	keeping up British morale during the London Blitz
nutrients	other nutrients	travel guide	journey through circulation system
stowaway	family	postcard	life on Henry Hudson's famous voyage
plant	soil	thank you note	soil's role in plant's life
Louis Pasteur	other scientists	memo	convincing them to pasteurize milk to prevent disease
Frederick Douglass	Harriett Beecher Stowe	book review	reactions to Uncle Tom's Cabin
parasite	host	love letter	explain relationship
Pablo Picasso	prospective employer	resumé	qualifications as an artist
antibiotic	other antibiotics	e-mail message	how to stop bacteria
dietitian	patients	Web page	heart-healthy diet
arteries	cholesterol	complaint	effects of fatty foods
person	public	editorial	ethics of cloning

Strategies: Key Sentences

❖ Key Sentences

Often students have a tendency to start most of their sentences the same way rather than using variety. One fun way to eliminate this tendency is with the key sentences organizer on page 127. Have the students record sentences that they want to include in a composition. Each statement must start with a different letter of the alphabet. Set a limit, such as at least 12 or 15 sentences. Then have the students organize their sentences into four or five paragraphs. Not only will students enjoy this challenge, their compositions will improve!

Directions: Write sentences about your topic, starting each one with a different letter. You may use words that begin with "ex" for the "X" sentence

A	Asa Philip Randolph was given the NAACP's highest award, the Spingarn Medal, in 1942.
B	Born in 1889, Asa Philip Randolph became a leading proponent for laborer's rights during the first half of the 20th century.
C	Crescent Beach, Florida, is the birthplace of one of the most influential people in the American labor movement.
D	During World War II, black workers were mistreated by the defense industry.
E	Employment discrimination was banned in the defense industry and government in June 1941 as a result of Randolph's efforts.
F	
G	
H	However, President Roosevelt took no action.
I	In 1957 the AFL-CIO, the largest American labor union, made Randolph the vice president.
J	
K	
L	
M	
N	No longer could jobs be withheld based on a person's race, creed, color, or national origin.
O	Outraged, Randolph threatened to fill the capital with 100,000+ blacks in a mass protest.
P	President Roosevelt established the Fair Employment Practices Committee.
Q	
R	Randolph asked President Franklin D. Roosevelt to put a stop to the discrimination against black workers.
S	
T	The largest black labor union—railway porters—elected Randolph as their president in the 1920s.
U	
V	
W	
X	
Y	Yearning for more progress, Randolph organized a 1963 march in Washington, D.C., to protest ongoing injustices to blacks.
Z	

Strategies: Key Sentences *(cont.)*

Graphic Organizer

A	
B	
C	
D	
E	
F	
G	
H	
I	
J	
K	
L	
M	
N	
O	
P	
Q	
R	
S	
T	
U	
V	
W	
X	
Y	
Z	

Strategies: Magnet Summaries

✣ Magnet Summaries

With this variation of Magnet Summaries (Buehl, 2001), students identify facts related to magnet words (key terms) in a text. They record the magnet word and related facts onto a magnet and use them to write a concise summary on the bar of steel.

1. Introduce the technique by leading a discussion of the interaction of a magnet and steel. Present this analogy: Just as magnets are drawn to steel, magnet words draw facts to them.

2. Choose three magnet terms or phrases. Choose terms or phrases to which many facts can be applied. In this example, the magnet is American immigration.

3. Distribute copies of the graphic organizer on page 129. On the overhead, display a transparency of the graphic organizer showing the first magnet word you've chosen. Have students write it between the prongs of the magnet. Then ask students to recall important details from a reading that relate to that magnet word. Allow them to look at or, if necessary, reread parts of the passage.

4. Ask students to offer examples of words or phrases they want to write on the prongs of the magnet. Write these on your overhead magnet as they do the same on theirs.

5. When you have written between four and seven details for the magnet word, ask the class to generate a brief summary on the bar of steel using all the words on the magnet.

6. Display the other magnet words you've chosen and let students complete the graphic organizer independently.

7. Extend this activity by having students use the summaries they wrote on the bars of steel to develop a three-paragraph summary and write it on the back of the graphic organizer.

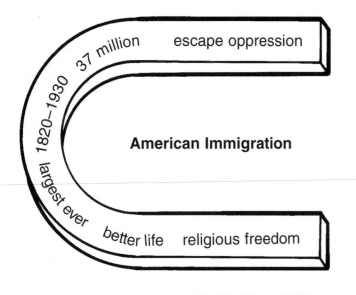

> escape oppression
> 37 million
> 1820–1930
> largest ever
> better life   religious freedom
>
> **American Immigration**

> Thirty-seven million people migrated to the United States from Europe and Africa between 1820–1930. This is the biggest human migration in recorded history. Although the Africans came involuntarily as slaves, the Europeans came to seek a better life and religious freedom.

Strategies: Magnet Summaries *(cont.)*

Graphic Organizers

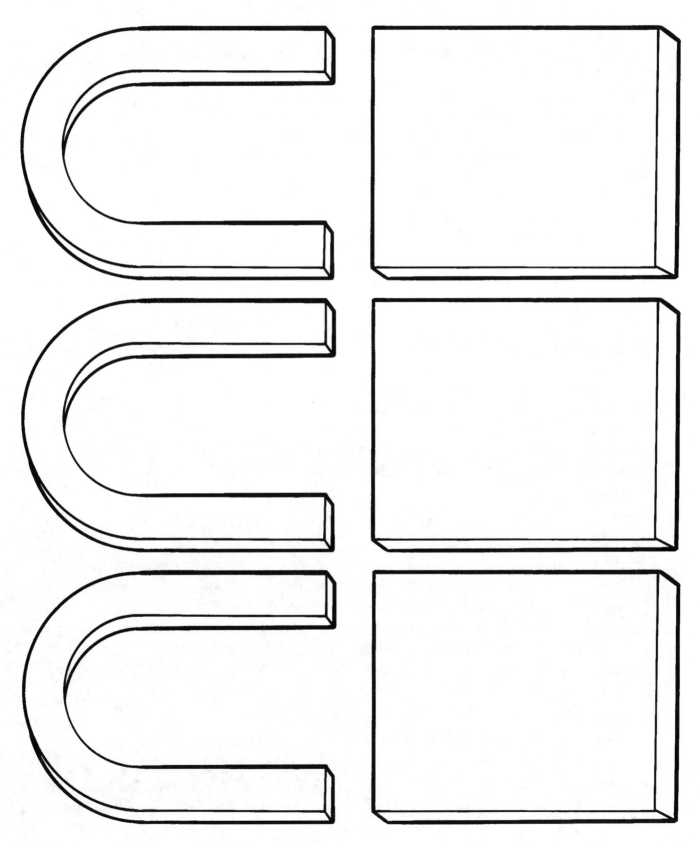

Strategies: Biopoems; Summary Frame

✛ Biopoems

Students can demonstrate their knowledge of famous people through biopoems (Gere, 1985).
Biopoems follow this format:

Line 1—Person's first name
Line 2—Four character traits
Line 3—Relative of (wife, husband, daughter, son, mother, father, sister, brother)
Line 4—Lover of (list three people or things to which the person is devoted)
Line 5—Who feels/felt (list three emotions)
Line 6—Who needs/needed (list three items)
Line 7—Who fears/feared (list three items)
Line 8—Who wants/wanted to see (list three items)
Line 9—Resident of (birthplace, where spent most of life, or residence at time of death)
Line 10—Person's last name

Here is an example of a biopoem about a famous American.

Abraham
Intelligent, stressed, determined, brave
Husband of Mary Todd
Lover of his family, books, and the United States of America
Who felt depressed, determined, and courageous
Who needed equality, justice, and cooperation
Who feared a divided union, a long war, and slavery
Who wanted to see an end to the Civil War, one nation, and freedom for all
Resident of Illinois
Lincoln

✛ Summary Frame

Before reading a nonfiction passage, provide students with copies of the blank summary frame on
page 131. Have the students write their response after the "know" statement. After the students
complete the reading, they complete the frame. The following is an example:

Before I started reading about <u>the Black Plague</u>, I knew <u>it was a fatal disease that had killed a
lot of the European population. People knew little about germs or sanitary conditions</u>.

In the article, <u>I learned the Plague occurred during 1347–1351 and killed 50,000 people in
Paris alone! Nobody knows the exact death toll because records weren't kept, but an
estimated 1/3 of Europe's whole population perished</u>.

I also learned <u>it was caused by a germ carried by the fleas that lived on rats</u>.

I was surprised <u>to find out that right before the Plague began people had killed off most of the
cats, believing that they were satanic. Since the cats had kept the rat population in check,
this meant that there were more rats than ever. If there had only been more cats, the
Plague would not have been as bad</u>.

Strategies: Summary Frame *(cont.)*

Graphic Organizer

Before I started reading about _____, **I knew**

_____

_____

_____

In the article, I learned_____

_____

_____

_____

_____

I also learned _____

_____

_____

I was surprised _____

_____

_____

_____

Strategies: Guided Reading

✢ Guided Reading Procedure

The Guided Reading Procedure (Manzo & Manzo, 1997) teaches students how to create an outline of expository text.

1. Select a passage. In the example given here, you might say, "Read this article to find out all you can about komodo dragons. Then on the overhead I will record what each of you recalls."

2. Students read the passage silently to themselves

3. Reconvene the class and ask, "What do you recall?"

4. Record all student responses, without regard for accuracy and without comment. Students cannot refer to the passage.

5. Students reread the passage again. This time give them only half the prior length of time. For example, if you gave 10 minutes for the first reading, give five for the second.

6. Reconvene the class and ask for if anyone knows additional information to add. At this point all errors should get corrected.

7. Tell students that they are going to put what they learned into an informal outline. Ask them to suggest category headings and organize the information underneath them.

8. Have the students place the passage and their outlines facedown on their desks and answer four comprehension questions that you have prepared in advance. You can collect the papers to check for understanding or as a quiz grade. Here's an example:

One of the world's scariest animals is the komodo dragon. They are the biggest lizards in the world, growing up to 10 feet (3 m) long and weighing up to 300 pounds (136 kg). Their bodies have thick, dark scales that look like a knight's armor. They have sharp, jagged teeth and claws the length of a human adult's longest finger. Dragons flick their forked tongue to smell for prey.

Komodo dragons are good hunters. They can run up to 10 miles per hour (16 kph) to get their prey. Then they unhinge their jaws so they can swallow pieces of meat that are bigger than their own heads. This lets them eat large animals such as deer, wild pigs, cattle, and water buffalo. They will also eat any human being they can catch.

Komodo dragons live in burrows. They also dig deep holes in the ground to bury about two dozen eggs. After eight months the baby dragons hatch and dig themselves out of their nest. They must hide from adult dragons—including their own parents—who will eat them. The babies soon learn to stay up in trees and come down only to eat. Their food is the scraps left after all the adults have finished eating.

The dragons live only on Komodo Island, located between Australia and Southeast Asia. Today they are endangered because humans have wiped out much of their prey.

Strategies: Guided Reading *(cont.)*

Teacher: "Without looking at the passage, tell me all that you can recall. I will write the items on the board." Here's the class's list:

- biggest lizards in the world
- weigh up to 300 pounds
- eat meat
- deer is prey
- thick, dark scales
- endangered due to humans
- people killed off prey

- grow to 10 feet
- hunter
- burrows for eggs
- forked tongue
- long claws
- live in burrows
- babies hide in treetops

- babies eat leftovers
- sharp, jagged teeth
- eat water buffalo
- run up to 10 mph
- babies afraid of adults
- unhinges jaws to eat big things

Teacher: "Let's write an outline using the information we have learned. First let's group the items we've listed into several categories." The students chose four categories: physical appearance, carnivore, reproduction, and endangered. Then they move the items they've recalled to fit under one of those four categories.

Physical Appearance

- biggest lizards in the world
- grow up to 10 feet long/300 pounds
- have thick, dark scales and long claws
- have a forked tongue and sharp, jagged teeth

Carnivore

- run up to 10 miles per hour to catch prey
- unhinge jaws to swallow big pieces of meat (deer and water buffalo)

Reproduction

- dig deep burrows for homes and also to bury eggs
- baby dragons are on their own; they avoid adults by hiding in treetops
- they eat leftovers from adult kills

Endangered

- live only on Komodo Island
- humans have killed their prey

Teacher: "Please turn the passage and your outline facedown. Take out a piece of paper and answer the four questions I am writing on the board."

1. What is unique about komodo dragons?

   Komodo dragons are the largest lizards in the world, weighing up to 300 pounds and growing up to 10 feet long. They live only on Komodo Island.

2. How do komodo dragons eat pieces of meat that are larger than their own heads?

   Their prey is large animals, so they can unhinge their jaws to eat pieces of meat that are bigger than their own heads.

3. How do komodo dragons take care of their young?

   They don't take care of their young. They will eat any babies they catch.

4. Are komodo dragons in jeopardy? Why or why not?

   Yes, komodo dragons are in danger of becoming extinct because they live only on one island and humans have depleted their food supply.

Strategies: Essay Templates; Dissecting Essay Questions

❖ Essay Templates

Teach students to write coherent essays with a template (Buehl, 2001). Ask an question followed by a paragraph with ideas stated in logical, sequential order but with blanks for key information. Students copy the entire template onto another paper, filling in the blanks. The blanks are not short answer, but often stand for a sentence or two.

Essay Question: What were the problems of the Great Depression, and what was done to solve them?

Answer Template: The Great Depression was caused by several problems in the American economy. One problem was <u>that banks had made bad loans. When people didn't pay back, the banks ran out of money and closed</u>. <u>This meant that people lost their life savings.</u> Another problem was <u>that the stock market crashed, bankrupting businesses and investors</u>. <u>Unemployment</u> was an additional hardship because <u>one out of every three workers lost their jobs</u>. <u>The government</u> tried to solve these problems with <u>the New Deal</u>. It also attempted to <u>reduce unemployment by creating government jobs (WPA and CCC)</u>. In addition, <u>the Social Security Act was enacted to keep people from becoming destitute</u>.

❖ Dissecting Essay Questions

After students have achieved success with essay templates, introduce Question Dissection (Williams, 1986). Students pick apart an essay question by asking a series of questions to form a plan.

Example: Describe three modes of transportation used in the United States during the 1800s.

The student asks the following questions:

1. What is the subject?
2. What is the active verb?
3. What is it asking you to do?
4. How many examples are needed?
5. Must the examples be written in order?

Correct response:

modes of transportation
describe
give an explanation or description
three
no

Students need to recognize the verbs frequently used in essay questions and what each means:

These verbs	Need this type of response
describe, define, explain, illustrate	give an explanation
compare, contrast, distinguish, identify the differences, state the similarities	compare/contrast
explain, interpret, discuss, caused, relate	show cause & effect
critique, evaluate, defend, justify, prove	defend a theory, hypothesis, or opinion

Teach students to rewrite the test question as the opening sentence of their essays. Doing this will help to snap students out of their writer's block or fear of beginning. For this example:

Three modes of transportation used in the United States during the 1800s were . . .

Strategies: Letters to the Editor; Defend Your Stance

✥ Letters to the Editor

Students can learn a great deal about point of view by writing letters about issues from different points of view. For example, each student can write three letters to the editor about the same subject: building a jail on county-owned land adjacent to the school. The first letter should be from a parent's point of view, the second from a county legislator's points of view, and the third from the student's own point of view.

✥ Defend Your Stance

Make a statement and ask the students to take a stand and explain their viewpoints in writing. For example: "In America only police, military, and security workers should have access to guns." Lead them to see that if they write an article about this topic that it would be impossible to prevent their biases from creeping in and that this happens to most nonfiction authors. After reading a nonfiction passage in which you detect author bias or values, select one or more of these journal questions to prompt students to reflect upon an author's bias and personal values:

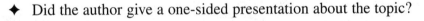

- ✦ Did the author give a one-sided presentation about the topic?

- ✦ How does the author feel about this topic? What words or phrases in the article make you think so?

- ✦ Who is the author's audience? Does this affect the author's tone?

- ✦ If you were writing an article about this same topic, how would yours differ from this one?

- ✦ Are there any places in the article where you wish that you could have asked the author a question? Where? Why?

- ✦ Do you agree with the author's stance?

Strategies: Opinion and Support Diamond

✣ Opinion and Support Diamond

This graphic organizer visually displays for students the relationship between a hypothesis or opinion, the underlying facts, evidence, examples, and the conclusions drawn. A theory or opinion is held up (supported) by facts, evidence, and examples; and the conclusions drawn come from the supporting information.

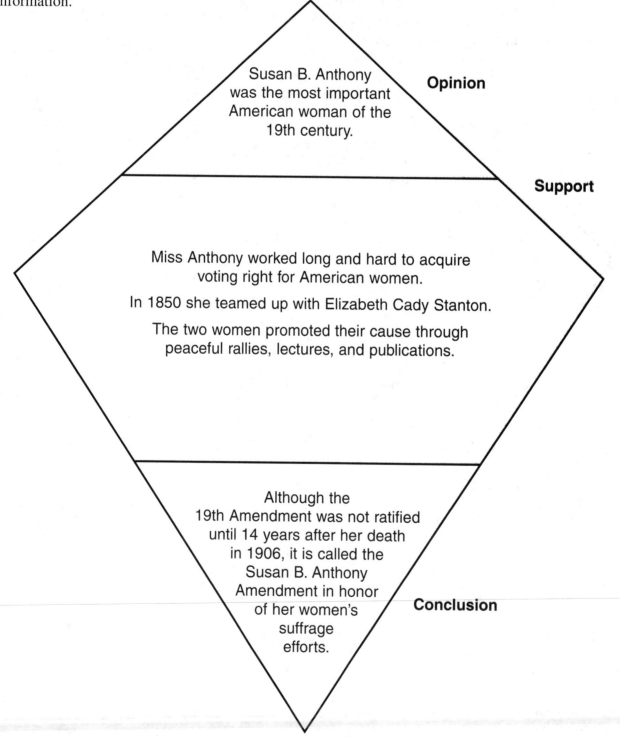

Susan B. Anthony was the most important American woman of the 19th century.

Opinion

Support

Miss Anthony worked long and hard to acquire voting right for American women.

In 1850 she teamed up with Elizabeth Cady Stanton.

The two women promoted their cause through peaceful rallies, lectures, and publications.

Although the 19th Amendment was not ratified until 14 years after her death in 1906, it is called the Susan B. Anthony Amendment in honor of her women's suffrage efforts.

Conclusion

Strategies: Opinion and Support Diamond *(cont.)*

Graphic Organizer

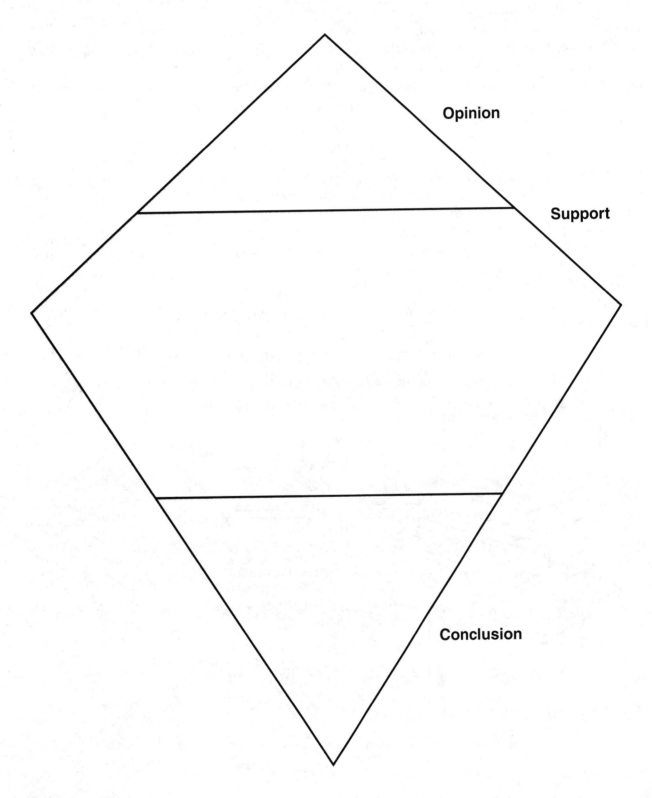

Opinion

Support

Conclusion

Introduction to Section 7: Researching Nonfiction

Research always begins with a question. Think about when you've conducted research in your daily life: it was always when you had a question. Adults research the housing market before buying or selling a house. They may read *Consumer Reports* before deciding on a vehicle model to consider for purchase. People investigate a variety of insurance companies for the best benefits or look into several charities to determine which one shares their objectives. These real questions demand real answers. Suppose that you were considering having corrective laser surgery on your eyes. For your primary research, you would talk to ophthalmologists and other people who have had the procedure done. You might visit a clinic to watch the procedure being done. For your secondary research, you might conduct Internet research and read pamphlets and magazine articles on the subject.

In pursuit of a real question, you learn a great deal. You want to afford your students the same opportunity to do genuine research. Therefore, allow them to formulate and pursue their own research questions. Your students will learn the same research skills with less resistance by pursuing a topic of their choice. This also makes their experience more meaningful, enjoyable, and memorable, and can make a crucial difference in both the attitude and effort of the students who struggle or feel disenfranchised. So encourage a student to investigate and prepare research materials about football cards, if that's what really interests him. If your district insists that students prepare a research project on a specific subject, try to define that topic as broadly as possible to give students latitude in finding a question that they really want to investigate. For example, you can have your students pursue a topic of their choice under a broad curricular area such as the Pacific Ocean or inventions.

138

Strategies: Inquiry-Based Research; Research Questions

✢ Inquiry-Based Research;

Stephanie Harvey (1998) outlines the components of inquiry-based research:

1. Decide on a topic.

2. Come up with three meaningful questions about the subject. Think of one or two theories to answer each question.

3. Gather information from a variety of secondary sources (books, magazine articles, computer resources, videos, the Internet, etc.), complemented by at least one primary source (interviews, field trips, museum displays, surveys, correspondence with experts, etc.).

4. Organize, interpret, and draw conclusions about the information obtained.

5. Share these conclusions with others.

✢ Helping Students Establish Research Questions

Most students can identify a topic of interest. For those who have difficulty, one of the best ways to guide students to find research topics that interest them is to refer them to their own unanswered questions in their learning logs.

After deciding on a topic, students need questions about it. Questions inspire research for a personal, real purpose—not just because the teacher assigned it. Thought-provoking questions are usually the most suitable for inquiry. Give students adequate time to think of these questions. Often at the start of their research they don't possess enough background knowledge to pose meaningful questions. Some may struggle to establish questions and need your guidance. If this happens, offer these questions and tell them to choose those that interest them as a framework for their projects.

◆ What is the purpose of _____?

◆ What is the structure of _____?

◆ What are the strengths of _____?

◆ What are the weaknesses of _____?

◆ I wonder why _____?

◆ Why does _____ matter?

◆ Why should we learn about _____?

◆ What could happen if we didn't learn about _____?

Strategies: The Research Process; Research Time Line

✥ The Research Process

The research process follows these steps:

1. **Planning**—Establish deadlines for inquiry questions, information gathering, categorizing and classifying, first draft, second draft, final copy, and the final publication/presentation.

2. **Questioning**—Students determine questions they want to investigate and then ask, "Where should I go or whom should I ask for information?"

3. **Gathering and recording information**—Students start with an encyclopedia entry to get a broad overview and essential background information. Encourage all of your students—even those in middle school—to read picture books. These books often contain wonderful photos or illustrations. This also enables below-grade-level readers to read them without drawing attention to themselves. Students should use both primary (at least one) and secondary sources. Primary sources include personal letters, interviews, surveys, and trips (to farms, museums, etc). Secondary sources include print, electronic, or other media. For grades 4–6, require that students use at least four total resources; for grades 7–8, require that students use a minimum of six total resources. Students should record information in any way that appeals to them.

4. **Analyzing**—Students determine what information to include and the order of presentation.

5. **Putting it all together**—Students establish a format for their presentations (written report, PowerPoint slide show, guided imagery, jackdaw, etc.). This step includes writing/creating, revising, critiquing, and editing to perfect the final product.

6. **Sharing findings with others**—Students publish or present their final products to classmates, another class, parents, administrators, or volunteer adults.

✥ Research Time Line

To do in-depth inquiry projects will take your most precious resource: time. However, it is time well spent. Your students will probably complete only two or three inquiry projects during the academic year. Keep in mind that two well-done, in-depth projects are more educationally advantageous to your students than four hastily done ones.

The time line below works well for a research project. To help students pace themselves, set the following deadlines:

- ◆ selection of a topic and inquiry questions (*beginning of week 2*)

- ◆ end of research phase (*middle of week 4*)

- ◆ first draft (*end of week 4*)

- ◆ second draft (*end of week 5*)

- ◆ final draft (*end of week 6*)

- ◆ presentation (*weeks 7 & 8*)

Strategies: Research Time Line *(cont.)*

Week 1

Share inquiry projects from former students. Expose students to a wide variety of topics by reading aloud from nonfiction trade books, newspapers, magazines, and Web sites. Let students choose materials to read in order to find topics that interest them. Encourage them to read books below their instructional reading level: this enables them to review the most topics before selecting one. Provide nonfiction reading materials below grade level, at grade level, and above grade level. You may be able to enlarge your classroom book selection through the school library or even the public library. Some public libraries will loan large quantities of materials to teachers for up to 30 days for classroom use.

Create a contract that states the student's name, topic, three inquiry questions (emphasize that they cannot be mere yes or no questions), and the five deadline dates. Send the contract home and ask both students and parents to sign and return it to you.

✦ ✦ ✦

Week 2

The contract is due. As students begin their research, teach them to skim material before deciding to read something in depth. Demonstrate a variety of note-taking strategies, including the use of note cards and graphic organizers. Let each student choose any method that works for him or her. Post an example of proper citation form for bibliographic entries.

✦ ✦ ✦

Weeks 3 and 4

Students search for information and take notes. They may generate additional questions and strive to answer those, too. Meet with each student at least once during this time (choose those who appear to be struggling first) to evaluate what, if any, interventions may be necessary to promote success. Have students write brief summaries of their anticipated presentations to include in the invitations that you send out. Establish a presentation schedule and send out invitations. The students submit their first drafts at the end of week 4.

✦ ✦ ✦

Weeks 5 and 6

During this time students engage in peer editing and work at revising their projects (written reports, multimedia presentations, etc). The second draft is due by the end of week 5. After additional polishing and revisions, the final project is due at the end of week 6.

✦ ✦ ✦

Weeks 7 and 8

Allot each student up to 10–15 minutes to present his or her final project.

Primary-Source Strategies: Surveys

Professional interviewers rarely ask questions that can be answered yes or no. Instead, they ask questions that will draw an extended response. Before your students engage in primary research, model an interview with another adult for your class if at all possible. Demonstrate good interview techniques by asking such questions as these:

1. How did you become an expert (or become interested) in your field?

2. What did you do in order to learn more about it?

3. Do you have any personal experiences or interesting stories you can share about your work?

4. Can you recommend any books that you think I should read about this topic?

5. Is there anything else you would recommend I investigate—videos or other materials?

6. Can you think of anyone else to whom I should talk about this topic?

Follow up by having each student choose an area in which he or she has expertise (such as cartoons or skateboarding) and conduct mock interviews, with students practicing interview questions or techniques on each other. Once your students know how to ask the right kinds of questions of experts, help them to find the experts by using the phone book.

1. Discuss the purpose and organization of each part and where to look for information (the White Pages are used if you already know the person or organization's name).

2. Show the students the guide words used to organize information in the Yellow Pages.

3. The information is there; the challenge is to find the correct label. Assist them in thinking of multiple guide words for a category. For example, a student was researching landfills and wanted to talk with someone in a garbage collection company for his primary research. After looking in the Yellow Pages under "trash" and "garbage" and finding nothing, he was stumped. His teacher suggested looking under "refuse." It wasn't there, but under refuse they found the notation to look under "rubbish collection."

✛ Surveys

Some students will conduct surveys for their primary source information. They should select an audience (their class, the entire fifth grade in your school, a neighborhood) and choose three questions that can be answered with a simple yes or no. To carry out this research, the students need to know how to record responses with tick marks, tabulate the responses, and then create graphs or percentages to show the results. Be sure to provide examples and an explanation of when and why to use each kind of graph:

✦ Pie graphs show parts of a whole.

✦ Bar graphs and pictographs are useful in comparing items.

✦ Line graphs show a trend or changes over time.

Conclusions drawn from a survey must be included in the final project.

Primary-Source Strategies: Creating Graphics; A Community of Learners

✤ Creating Graphics

Students enjoy demonstrating their knowledge by creating graphs or charts. After researching the elements of Earth's crust, a student used a computer to generate this graph:

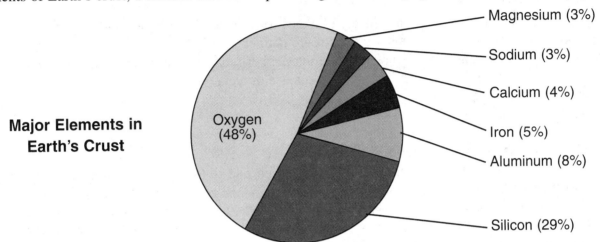

Major Elements in Earth's Crust

Oxygen (48%)

Magnesium (3%)

Sodium (3%)

Calcium (4%)

Iron (5%)

Aluminum (8%)

Silicon (29%)

✤ A Community of Learners

Research thrives in a community of learners. Think of how you've asked others for recommendations on a good plumber, podiatrist, etc. Word of mouth helps small businesses to thrive or fail. In addition, first-hand information is often the most interesting. Capitalize on this by creating a bulletin board that encourages students and staff to share their expertise. Put the bulletin board in a central place in the school to which both students and staff have access. The students write their areas of inquiry, their names, teacher's name, and grade in one column. The second column provides space for others to respond with their name and how to contact them.

Can You Tell Me About:	Yes! Here's how to contact me:
orangutans Shauna Williams, Mr. Smith, gr. 5	Mrs. DeSalma Leave me a message in my mailbox in the main office.
steam engines Rja Adul, Ms. Sadowski, gr. 4	Mr. Morton, custodian Come see me. I'm in my office every day before school.
hang gliding Damon Walker, Mrs. Argast, gr. 6	Yvette Fernandez, Mr. Yunker's grade 6 Call me at 555-0987 after school.

You may be surprised at how much "expertise" exists within your school family. Someone's dad may work with the snakes at a local zoo. A fifth grader may have researched and prepared a presentation on hot air balloons in fourth grade. The librarian may be a motorcycle enthusiast.

Send home a monthly notice with a list of topics that haven't received any responses. In this way, you can involve parents and extended relatives by notifying them of a need for expertise they may possess. Not only is this good public relations, it lets students see those around them in a new light. Everyone is an expert at something.

Secondary-Source Strategies: Evaluating Sources; Knowing Where to Look

❖ Evaluating Sources

Since most of your students will immediately gravitate toward the use of books and magazines, they need to know that books with old copyright dates are not necessarily bad; however, more recent information may have rendered them obsolete. Historical events are usually described accurately in outdated publications, but this often isn't so with science or technology. Also, make sure that your students realize that not everything is known or may ever be known about an ancient event or a person who lived long ago.

❖ Knowing Where to Look for Answers

Students need to know where to search for answers to their questions. Gather together a collection of different styles of expository text. Ask students to determine the common elements in all nonfiction books. Then have students identify possible questions that they might ask about each book (does it have an appendix, glossary, index, table of contents, illustrations, etc.), its probability of answering a certain type of question, and where to look in the book for the answer to a question. Show students how to quickly determine a source's potential usefulness in answering research questions by giving them a familiarity with book parts (Bamford & Kristo, 2000). A simple exercise can present this information to them:

Directions: The left column lists different parts of reference books. The right column has things you may need to find out. Draw a line to match the part of the book where you would most likely find the information.

Book part	You want to know
1. glossary	a. in what year the book was published
2. table of contents	b. whether George Eastman is mentioned in the book
3. copyright page	c. a list of the chapters in the book
4. index	d. how to find an article that was quoted in the book
5. appendix of maps	e. what the word "plateau" means
6. bibliography/sources	f. the geography of Mexico

(**Answers:** 1—e, 2—c, 3—a, 4—b, 5—f, 6—d)

Secondary-Source Strategies: Library; Computer; Organizing

✢ Using the Library for Research

Before embarking on a research project, distribute grid paper and take the students to the school library. Have each student make a map of the library, indicating where these things are located:

- ◆ nonfiction books
- ◆ fiction books
- ◆ CD-ROMs/videos
- ◆ encyclopedias

- ◆ biographies
- ◆ computers
- ◆ magazines
- ◆ unabridged dictionary

- ◆ thesaurus
- ◆ atlases, maps
- ◆ microfilm/fiche
- ◆ microfilm reader

✢ Using a Computer for Research

The Internet can consume too much time for too little benefit. Prevent this from happening to students by having them do Internet research only when:

- ◆ the information needs to be up-to-date (such as recent scientific discoveries of anti-cancer properties of an Amazon rain forest plant or innovations in electric-hybrid cars)

- ◆ they cannot locate much information in other sources

- ◆ they need information from distant experts and can find a way to contact them via the Web

- ◆ the topic is too new to be in many print sources (such as a possible vaccine for human papilloma virus)

Show students how to limit a cybersearch. For example, entering "accordion" as a topic may result in 235, 489 hits. Entering "manufacture of Werlitzer accordion" will result in fewer. They may also need guidance in choosing alternative key words to use as search descriptors.

Post key rings with index cards attached at the computer. On each index card, write the topic, URL, and a brief description of a Web site that you or a student has found helpful. Continue to add new cards, maintaining alphabetical order based on topic. As these key ring collections grow over time, they can save your students a lot of time.

✢ Organizing Materials

Use individual mini baskets or cubbies in which students may keep their research materials. Larger baskets are also ideal for text sets—nonfiction works about a particular topic written at a variety of reading levels (at, above, and below grade). If you purchase the small, laundry-style baskets, be sure to get the 14 ¾" L x 10 ¼" W x 4 ⅔" H size, because many nonfiction books tend to be large.

Secondary-Source Strategies: Recording Information; Sum-It-Up Chart

✛ Recording Information

Research means taking notes. Demonstrate several ways to take notes and let each student choose his or her favorite method. In addition to the Sum-It-Up, Inquiry, and K-W-L charts described in this section, refer to Key Word Notes (page 114) and Informal Notes Outline (page 112).

✛ Sum-It-Up Chart

A sum it up chart is a great way for students to record notes. A template is available on page 147. Have students use a separate Sum-It-Up chart for each reference work. Here's an example:

Who or What	American Colonists	Source
Did What	said they were independent from England	*2001 World Book Encyclopedia* on CD-ROM. Ivid Communications and IBM Corporation, 2001.
When	July 4, 1776	
Where	Philadelphia, Pennsylvania	
Why	they wanted their own government	
How	through the Declaration of Independence	

Write a paragraph that sums up the information in the chart:

The American colonists said that they were independent from England on July 4, 1776, in Philadelphia, Pennsylvania. The Declaration of Independence stated that they wanted their own government.

Secondary-Source Strategies: Sum-It-Up Chart *(cont.)*

Graphic Organizers

Sum It Up

Who or What		
Did What		
When		
Where		
Why		
How		

Write a paragraph that sums up the information in the chart._____

_____

_____

_____

Strategies: Inquiry Chart

✛ Inquiry Chart

When students complete an inquiry chart (Hoffman, 1992), they grow accustomed to looking at things from different perspectives. Inquiry charts also help students whose research reveals conflicting information. Model the inquiry chart with the whole class by making a transparency of page 149. Have students brainstorm three questions that they'd like answered and write them above the columns. Read aloud from three different sources and record the information from each source. After reviewing the information, write a one-sentence summary at the bottom of each column.

Inquiry Chart for the Loch Ness Monster

	Who has seen the monster?	What does it look like?	What do scientists think it is?	Other Interesting Facts
Source: *The Loch Ness Monster* by Ellen Rabinowich	—hundreds of Scottish people —three fishermen's boat was lifted out of the water while they were in it —Hugh Gray took first photo in 1933	—long neck —little head —two small horns —over 40 feet long —one or two humps on back	—a descendant of a plesiosaur (swimming dinosaur) —a huge sea cow (manatee) —an undiscovered sea serpent species	—Loch Ness is a very deep lake in Scotland —water is full of peat, which makes it hard to see anything (looks like coffee grounds!)
Source: *Monster Mysteries* by Rupert Matthews	—1934 "Surgeon's Photo" taken by R. Kenneth Wilson —1960 a family took 4 minutes of home video	—1975 photo shows vague outline of large animal with flippers	—an unknown worm species —a descendant of a plesiosaur	—no known victims injured by the creature called "Nessie" —plesiosaurs never lived in such cold water
Source: *2000 World Book Encyclopedia* CD-ROM	—first sighting reported in 565 A.D. by Saint Columbia —underwater photos taken in 1972 and 1975	—20 to 30 feet long —four flippers —long, slender neck —tiny head —between one and three humps	—a descendant of a plesiosaur —an unknown species of water snake	—in 1994 Dr. Wilson admitted the "Surgeon's Photo" was a fake
Summary	Hundreds of people and many photos seem to point to the reality of a Loch Ness monster.	Most people report that the creature has a long, thin neck; little head; a hump; and flippers.	Most scientists suggest that the Loch Ness monster is a plesiosaur.	Loch Ness's water makes it hard to find out anything for sure.

Inquiry charts show that sometimes "facts" are disputed. Let students know that some information has been lost forever. (For example, the exact date of Harriett Tubman's birth will never be known because records were not kept of slave births). Also, written materials are limited in length and often heavily edited. Thus, authors make choices about what information to include and what to omit. Review the completed inquiry chart, asking students these questions:

✦ What information did all the authors include? Why do you think this is?

✦ Which information did only one author include? Why do you think this is?

Strategies: Inquiry Chart *(cont.)*

Graphic Organizer

Inquiry Chart for _____

				Other Interesting Facts
Source:				
Source:				
Source:				
Summary				

Strategies: K-W-L Chart

⊹ K-W-L Chart

A K-W-L chart (Ogle, 1986) offers a good format for research notes. Distribute copies of page 151. Ask the students to write everything they already know about their topics in the "I Know" column. Have them each think of three research questions for their topics and record them in the "I Wonder" column. K-W-L charts enable you to maintain control over the research process by reviewing the students' charts at these critical points:

- ✦ beginning (check the "I Know" column)

- ✦ after they've established the three queries (look at the "I Wonder" column)

- ✦ about midway through the time allotted for research (look at the "I Learned" column)

This student has prepared a K-W-L chart about board games at the beginning of her inquiry project. She has written all she knows about board games, in the "I Know" column. In the "I Wonder" column, she has written four research questions followed by her theory in parentheses. She will fill in the "I Learned" column as she finds information.

I Know	I Wonder	I Learned
Board games have pieces, markers, etc., that you move around a board.	How is a board game developed? (*a bunch of people meet as a committee to come up with a board game and then it's field tested*)	
Board games I like: Monopoly, Payday, Clue, Guess Who, Chess	What makes a board game popular? (*easy to learn, inexpensive, pastime before radio and electronic entertainment was available*)	
My parents say that some of these same board games were around when they were kids.	What is the most popular board game of all time and why? (*checkers*)	
You usually need at least two people to play a board game.	What board game has been around the longest, how long has it been around, and why has it lasted? (*chess*)	

Strategies: K-W-L Chart *(cont.)*

Graphic Organizer

I Know	I Wonder	I Learned

Research Projects: Guided Imagery; Jackdaws

⁜ Guided Imagery

Students can develop guided imagery exercises (Gambrell, et al., 1987) about their topics. They learn a great deal both from preparing their own guided imagery exercises and experiencing each other's. Students are usually very attentive as a classmate guides them through his or her guided imagery exercise. Encourage students to develop their own ideas. You can also provide this list of ideas:

- ✦ writing and performing a skit or a puppet show (effective for biographies and historical events)

- ✦ having the rest of class wear blindfolds while a student talks them through a visualization of the topic (such as a day in the life of a polar bear)

- ✦ storytelling (without pictures) that includes important facts about the topic. Students may use cue cards but cannot read aloud.

- ✦ providing tactile props to help explain characteristics. A student reporting about eggs had each person in the class stick his or her hand through the lid of four different shoeboxes. Inside each was an example of a type of egg. One box had a hard-boiled chicken egg; another a jar of jelly (for fish, toad, and frog eggs); another had shampoo (for certain types of insect eggs); and the final box had a leaf with insect eggs actually implanted in it.

- ✦ writing a poem or song that includes all the pertinent information and performing it for the class

Ideas are only as limited as your students' imagination. For example, a fourth grader read about Johann Sebastian Bach, taught herself to play one of his easiest pieces on a laptop keyboard, and then performed it for her classmates. This gave them more genuine knowledge than just being told the fact that he is the father of Baroque music.

⁜ Jackdaws

A jackdaw is an unusual bird that collects anything it can carry and hoards it in its nest. As a project, a jackdaw is a collection of things related to a specific topic, often displayed in a shoebox. Jackdaws promote higher-level thinking skills in an enjoyable way. Students must prepare a short report explaining the selection of items in the jackdaw. To the right, is a student's jackdaw about the state of Arizona:

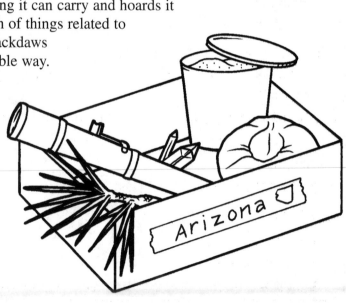

- ✧ cup of sand (desert)

- ✧ quartz (Petrified Forest)

- ✧ telescope (Lowell Observatory)

- ✧ pine twigs (Ponderosa pines)

- ✧ clay with crater (Barrington Crater)

Research Projects: Written Reports

✛ Written Reports

For strategies to teach students how to write nonfiction, refer to the Writing Nonfiction section on pages 120–137.

Suppose a student wants to write a captain's log of the 15th century Portugese explorer Vasco da Gama's historic voyage around the Cape of Good Hope. He or she can make the paper look old by "antiquing" it. Paper can be antiqued by gently wiping it all over with a wet black tea bag (herbal and green teas don't work), then drying it by laying it flat on a cookie sheet. Add little, brown age spots by sprinkling individual grains of instant coffee onto the paper while it's still damp. (This will cause tiny stains that give the paper an authentic look.) Handwriting looks more authentic than type on antiqued paper. Heavier paper can also be treated by carefully burning the edges. (This technique should be done with adult supervision before the paper has been written.)

Require students to include at least one visual in any written report. For example, a student can draw to scale (by hand or computer) a graph that depicts the size of the average adult human compared to the length of a blue whale; or include a drawing of a blue whale in its ocean habitat, surrounded by other creatures that share the depths with it (most are minuscule by comparison!).

Citing Sources

Use the following guidelines when citing sources for any research report. If a student uses a computer, the titles should be in italics. If the source list is handwritten, the titles must be underlined.

Book

Author's last name, first name. *Title*. Publisher, copyright date.

Example: Housel, Debra. *Developing Listening Skills*. Teacher Created Resources, 2001.

CD-ROM

Title of CD-ROM. CD-ROM. Publisher(s), date.

Example: *2001 World Book Encyclopedia*. CD-ROM. Ivid Communications and IBM Corporation, 2001.

Magazine or newspaper article

Author's last name, first name. "Title of article." *Title of Magazine*. Date: page numbers for article.

Example: Power, Brenda. "Talk in the Classroom." *Scholastic Instructor*.
    September 2001: 37–39.

Video/film

Title of film. Medium. Publisher, year. Length.

Example: *The Grizzlies*. Videotape. National Geographic Video, 1987. 60 minutes.

Web site

Name of Web site. URL.

Example: Teacher Created Resources. http://www.teachercreated.com

---

Introduction to Section 8: Assessing Nonfiction Comprehension

Every instructional activity your class does can be used for assessment. This section will provide you with additional ways to determine your students' educational progress.

The purpose of assessment is to let you know the specific instruction your students need. Assessment gives you a picture of the instructional needs of the class, increasing the productive use of instructional time because you don't spend time going over things that the class already knows. Authentic assessment lets you pinpoint each student's specific strengths, weaknesses, and misconceptions. This type of evaluation tells you, the student, and the parents more useful information than a "B+" or an "86." Some popular, authentic assessment tools include:

✦ portfolios

✦ performances

✦ scoring guides

✦ educator observation checklists and anecdotal records

✦ student self-assessment

Strategies: Performances

✛ Performances

Performances are tangible products such as tests, reports, projects, presentations, or oral summations. An example of a performance assessment is to tape each student individually reading an unfamiliar nonfiction piece aloud at four points during the school year (at the end of each quarter). At the same time have students do a writing sample. Store these performances in chronological order on a disk as a record of growth and learning to share with students, parents, and administrators.

Blachowicz and Ogle (2001) suggest recording a performance of students' metacognitive processes. This performance task can be done only after you have modeled the process of a think-aloud (see page 36). Tape record each student reading a nonfiction passage he or she has never seen before. Let the student preview the text (noting aloud the text features such as headings and graphs), then make a prediction and mention something already known about the topic. As the student reads aloud, he or she should stop and comment on the reading by musing aloud or asking questions. After the student finishes reading, he or she orally summarizes the passage.

Strategies: Portfolios; Scoring Guides; Checklists

✣ Portfolios

A portfolio is a collection of each student's work and academic development over time. Each student's portfolio showcases his or her best pieces of work throughout a school year. Make portfolios a collaborative effort between you and each student; decide together what to include. To reduce the bulk of a single portfolio, you may want separate portfolios for each student in each content area.

Portfolio pieces are limited only by space and imagination. They can include a graph of student progress (such as fluency in terms of words read per minute), journals, word problems, samples of a student's written work, videotapes, his or her portion of group projects, and computer-generated assignments (such as a PowerPoint™ presentation on a CD).

✣ Scoring Guides

Scoring guides provide a set of standards for measuring a student's skills. These evaluations allow you to assess each part of a student's work in order to arrive at an overall grade. Scoring guides provide an accurate measure of student performance. Prior to assigning a task, review the scoring guide with the students so that they know what's expected. These scoring guides are provided:

- ◆ **Oral Summation** (page 166)—Model for the students how to give an oral summary. Establish a system for randomly drawing students' names, such as craft sticks kept in a mug or names on slips of paper in a shoebox. After the class completes an expository reading, pick a student name and ask him or her to summarize or retell what's been read.

- ◆ **Written Summation** (page 167)—Allow no access to the text while the student is composing the retelling. Emphasize that ideas count much more than spelling or mechanics.

- ◆ **Discussion** (page 168)—Fill out this assessment for each student at least three times a year.

- ◆ **Research and Written Report** (page 169)

- ◆ **Research and Presentation** (page 170)

✣ Educator Observation and Checklists

Educator observation checklists help you to notice and record student behaviors that indicate competence or difficulty. A checklist gives you quick, easy documentation of the specific skills a student has mastered. The conclusions drawn from such checklists are consistent and reliable if you use many observations over a period of time. Checklists are a good way for you to show students the areas they still need to work on as well as those in which they excel. They also offer a meaningful way to discuss with parents the standards and benchmarks as they relate to their child's abilities. A comprehensive checklist of receptive skills (reading and listening) is provided on page 171, and an expressive skills (writing, speaking, and research) checklist is given on page 172.

Strategies: Self-Assessment; "Opportunities"; Cloze

⊹ Student Self-Assessment

Students need to take an active role in their own assessment. Asking students to evaluate their own performances enables them to identify what they've done well and what they could improve. Page 173 has two student self-assessment tools. Students complete the top self-evaluation form after a unit of nonfiction study. Students fill out the bottom self-evaluation form after completing a major project or report. You may want to send these self-evaluation forms home for parent signature or you may choose to store them in the students' portfolios.

⊹ "Opportunities"

You cannot hide from students when and how they will be evaluated. Yet many students feel anxious when told in advance that "this is a test" or "this is for a grade." One easy way to alleviate test anxiety is to always call tests "opportunities." Explain to the students that a test is merely an opportunity for them to show you what they know and for you to find out what you still need to teach. This simple explanation and renaming often goes a long way toward reducing your students' test anxiety.

⊹ Cloze

Assess comprehension with a cloze passage. Select a passage from an expository text the students have not read but that is about the topic you have been studying. Prepare a worksheet like the one below, omitting every tenth word. Make certain that you leave blanks that are all the same size. This activity forces them to rely heavily on context in order to select the correct word. Here's an example:

Six types of man-made satellites orbit our planet. Some satellites _____

oceans, icebergs, volcanoes, deserts, forest fires, and moving animal _____

such as killer whales. Spy satellites watch the movement _____ armies

and navies. Weather satellites record cloud movements and _____

speeds. Some satellites let vehicles know their exact position _____

the Earth. Others keep track of the stars, comets, and meteors. _____

satellite you use every day is called a communications _____ .

These satellites get signals from our computers, telephones, and _____

cameras and beam them back down to another computer, _____ ,

or television.

Maze practice, a variation on the cloze technique, offers an assessment of vocabulary learning. Eliminate some of the important concept words and offer three word choices for each deletion.

Rethinking Traditional Test Items: True/False; Multiple Choice

Does authentic assessment and the emphasis on standards mean that you should abandon objective tests? Definitely not. However, you do need to change objective test items to higher-level thinking tasks.

✛ True/False Items

True/false items become higher-level thinking assessments if you add a defense component. By requiring a written defense, students must explain their reasoning. For younger students, you may give partial credit for true/false. For older students give credit only when the student offers a valid explanation.

1. A mutated gene only produces a change in the first generation.

    False. A mutated gene is changed forever and may produce a change in the first generation or a subsequent generation. If the mutated gene is recessive, it may never produce a change at all.

2. Some mutations help organisms adapt to their environment.

    True. These mutations are often the basis of natural selection. The organisms with the new, better mutations are more apt to adapt to their environment and predators. This enables them to survive and produce young.

✛ Multiple-Choice Items

Require a written defense (see "True/False Items" above) or present a sentence along with a question that the students must interpret, as shown in this example:

When the vase broke, Diego's mother cried.
She thought that the vase was _____.

a. worthless

b. an heirloom

c. a fake

d. alive

Rethinking Traditional Test Items: Matching; Word Searches

❖ Matching

Give lists of incomplete statements in two columns so that students must first identify the word(s) to complete each statement before they can find the matches. For example:

__C__	1.	Many colonists died because they faced so many **problems**.	A.	Early settlers needed help from **Native Americans**.
__D__	2.	**Roanoke Island** is now called "The Lost Colony."	B.	**Diseases** killed many people in Europe.
__B__	3.	A lot of Native Americans died from the **diseases** European settlers brought brought with them.	C.	One of the **problems** colonists had to deal with was a lack of food when crops were poor.
__A__	4.	**Native Americans** lived in our country prior to the arrival of Christopher Columbus.	D.	One of the earliest European settlements, was **Roanoke Island**.

❖ Word Searches

Word searches are challenging when students must generate the words to be located. To avoid frustration for struggling readers, a caveat applies to word searches: words should not be written backwards. Only use a software program to generate a word search if it lets you control this feature. In this example, students must identify these words and then locate them in the puzzle: *problems, people, smallpox, before.*

1. One of the p_____ colonists had to deal with was a lack of food when crops were poor.

2. Roanoke Island is now called "The Lost Colony" because no one knows what happened to the p_____ who lived there.

3. Many Native Americans died from the deadly s_____ that European settlers unintentionally brought with them to the New World.

4. Native Americans lived here b_____ Christopher Columbus arrived.

```
P  E  O  P  L  E  F  A
A  B  C  R  D  E  G  B
H  I  J  O  K  M  L  D
L  P  R  B  T  A  B  P
S  M  A  L  L  P  O  X
U  T  B  E  F  O  R  E
V  W  X  M  Y  Z  A  B
C  D  E  S  F  G  I  H
```

Rethinking Traditional Test Items: Fill-in-the-Blanks

✣ Fill-in-the-Blanks

Beef up fill-in-the-blank items with analogies. Analogies allow students to find relationships and show you if they absorbed the overall ideas of a unit. You can prepare three types of analogies: straightforward analogies, analogies about broad concepts, and analogies using concepts from different content areas. When you write these analogies, be sure you are evaluating the things that matter most (concepts and ideas) over pieces of information like names, dates, and places. You may be surprised at the interesting relationships your students will find between things.

Straightforward Analogies

1. 25 is to 5 as 16 is to <u>4</u>

2. angle is to rectangle as curve is to <u>circle</u>

3. plus is to addition as minus is to <u>subtraction</u>

Analogies about Broad Concepts

1. Metamorphic is a type of rock created by heat and pressure.
Another type of rock is <u>igneous</u>, which is created by <u>magma cooling down</u>.

2. Weathering is the part of the rock cycle. It wears rocks down.
Another part of the rock cycle is <u>compacting</u>. It <u>hardens sediments into solid rock</u>.

Analogies Using Concepts from Different Content Areas

Provide a statement that follows this format: A _____ is like _____ because _____ .

For example, if your class is studying weather in science and time in math, you could give your students a statement such as this:

A *thermometer* is like a *clock* because   <u>they both measure things.</u>
<u>people check them often.</u>
<u>they both have a scale.</u>

Strategies: Equation

✧ Main-Idea and Supporting-Details Equation

Evaluate your students' ability to locate the main idea and find supporting details with the assessment tool on page 161. Provide the students with an unfamiliar passage taken from a nonfiction text at their independent reading level. Here's an example:

Read this passage. Fill in the three small boxes with the details that add up to the main idea. Write the main idea in the largest box.

Most metals rust when exposed to oxygen, but aluminum does not. Aluminum reacts with oxygen to form a tough surface film. This film keeps the aluminum from being eaten away by rust. This is why aluminum is often used to make cars and airplanes. It is also used as a building material.

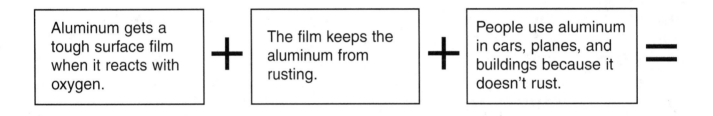

| Aluminum gets a tough surface film when it reacts with oxygen. | + | The film keeps the aluminum from rusting. | + | People use aluminum in cars, planes, and buildings because it doesn't rust. | = |

Aluminum does not rust when exposed to oxygen.

Strategies: Equation *(cont.)*

Graphic Organizer

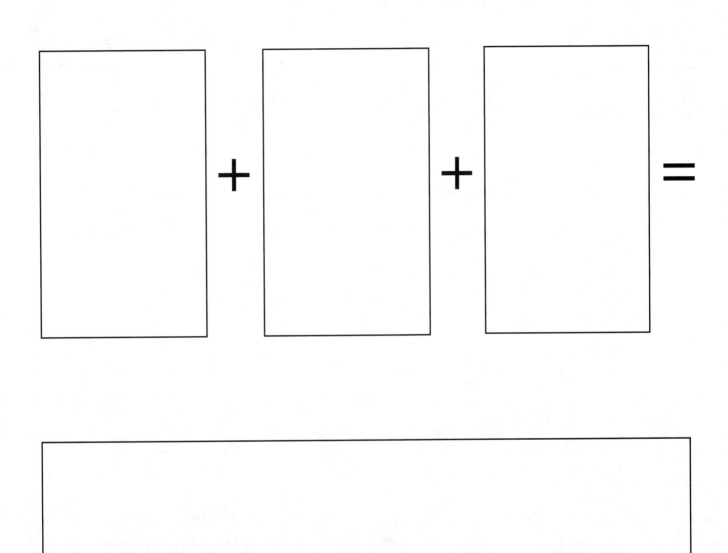

Strategies: Vocabulary into Essay

❖ Vocabulary into Essay

Vocabulary into Essay (Nichols, 1985) offers a good evaluation tool. For example, after learning about measurement, give the students the words in the box and three categories (in bold print):

liquid	yard(s)	cup(s)	quart(s)
gallon(s)	inch(es)	distance	width
foot	ounce(s)	heavy	length
mile(s)	pound(s)	pint(s)	height

Linear Measure	**Weight**	**Volume**
yards	heavy	liquid
inches	ounces*	cups
distance	pounds	quarts
width		pints
length		gallons
foot		
miles		
height		

*A student may put this under "Volume" if he or she does not understand the difference between ounces and fluid ounces.

Paragraphs

Linear measure tells you the length, width, or height of something. It can also be used to measure distance. Linear measure uses inches, feet, yards, and miles. There are 12 inches in one foot and three feet in one yard.

Weight tells you how heavy something is. Weight is measured in ounces and pounds. There are 16 ounces in one pound.

Volume tells you the amount of a liquid. Volume is measured in cups, pints, quarts, and gallons. There are two cups in one pint and four cups in one quart. Four quarts make a gallon.

Strategies: Vocabulary into Essay *(cont.)*

Graphic Organizer

Directions: Put each word in the box into one of the three groups below. Then write a paragraph using all the words in the first group. Write another paragraph using all the words in the second group. Do the same for a third paragraph.

Paragraphs: _____

_____

_____

_____

_____

_____

_____

_____

_____

Strategies: Herringbone

✢ Herringbone

A graphic organizer that allows students to quickly display their knowledge of who, what, when, where, why, and how is the herringbone (Tierney, Readence & Dishner, 1990), named for a fish skeleton. A herringbone graphic organizer is provided on page 165. This is how a completed herringbone would look:

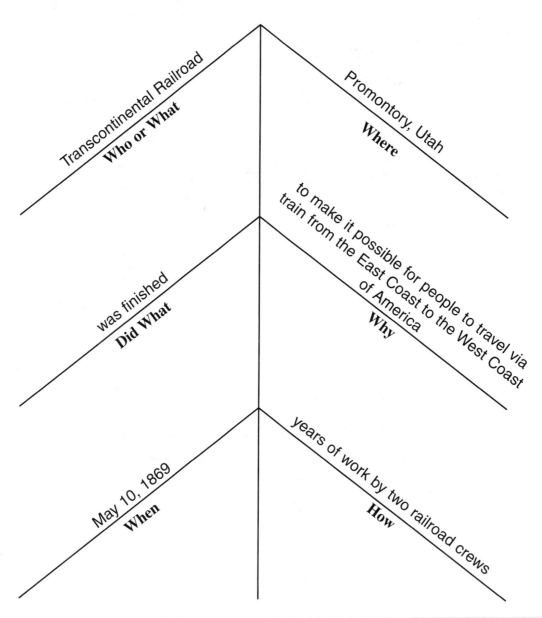

Summary:

The Transcontinental Railroad was completed on May 10, 1869, in Promontory, Utah. Building it had taken years of work and two separate railroad crews. One crew had started laying tracks at the East Coast heading west, and one had started laying tracks at the West Coast heading east. The Transcontinental Railroad made it possible to travel by train across the entire width of America.

Strategies: Herringbone *(cont.)*

Graphic Organizer

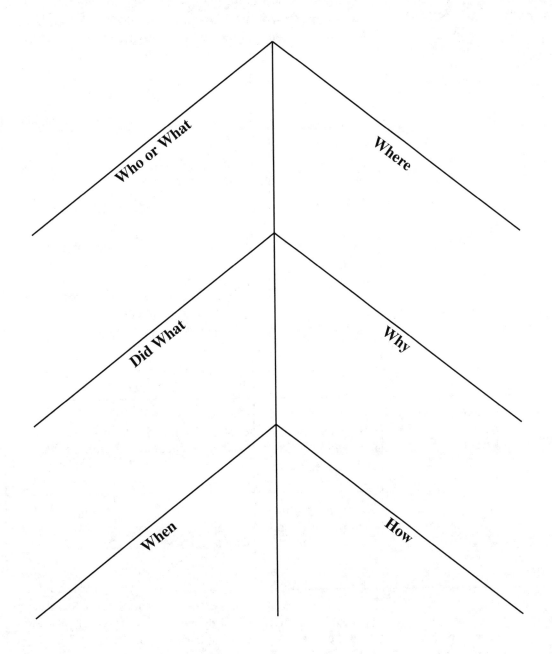

Summary:

Scoring Guide—Oral Summation

	Excellent (3 pt.)	Satisfactory (2 pt.)	Needs to Improve (1 pt.)	Poor (0 pt.)	Points
Topic	Identifies even unstated main idea(s) independenly.	Identifies the main idea(s) independently.	Can only identify main idea(s) with teacher prompts.	Cannot identify main idea(s) with teacher prompts.	
Details	Identifies all supporting details independently.	Identifies most of the supporting details.	Can identify all supporting details with teacher prompts.	Cannot identify all the supporting details with teacher prompts.	
Organization	Retells only relevant information in a logical, organized way.	Retells mostly relevant information in a logical, organized way with only one digression.	Includes irrelevant information and wanders from ending to beginning to middle and back again.	Retelling is illogical and haphazard; digresses from the topic.	
Sequence	States the events in the correct order.	States the events in order with some minor inaccuracies.	Can only state the events in order with teacher guidance.	Cannot state the events in order with teacher guidance.	
Concepts	Groups all similar concepts together.	Groups most similar concepts together.	Can group similar concepts together only with teacher's help.	Cannot group similar concepts together.	
Questions	Can answer all of the questions about the text.	Can answer most of the questions asked about the text.	Can answer questions about the text by looking back into the passage.	Cannot answer questions even when referring to the passage.	
				Total	

Overall Assessment Score: _____

Scoring Instructions: Score 3 points for each Excellent, 2 for each Satisfactory, 1 for every Needs to Improve, and 0 for every Poor. Total the points column and divide by 6 (the number of areas evaluated) for an overall assessment score.

Scoring Guide—Written Summation

	Excellent (3 pt.)	Satisfactory (2 pt.)	Needs to Improve (1 pt.)	Poor (0 pt.)	Points
Topic	Includes even unstated main idea(s) independently.	Includes the main idea(s).	Writes about theme without clearly identifying the main idea(s).	Does not write about the theme.	
Details	Includes all supporting details.	Includes most of the supporting details.	Includes one supporting detail and some irrelevant information.	Does not include any supporting details or includes only irrelevant information.	
Organization	Writes only relevant information in a logical, organized way.	Writes mostly relevant information in a logical, organized way with only one digression.	Includes irrelevant information and wanders from ending to beginning to middle and back again.	Paper is illogical and haphazard; digresses from the topic.	
Sequence	States the events in the correct order.	States most of the events in order with some minor inaccuracies.	States some of the events in order.	Does not state the events in order with teacher guidance.	
Concepts	Groups all similar concepts together.	Groups most similar concepts together.	Groups similar concepts together only with teacher's help.	Cannot group similar concepts together.	
Grammar	Always uses capitals, complete sentences, and punctuation accurately.	Often uses capitals; has one sentence fragment or run-on.	Uses some capitals; includes sentence fragments and/or run-ons.	Uses capitals sporadically and writes mostly sentence fragments and run-ons.	
				Total	

Overall Assessment Score: _____

Scoring Instructions: Score 3 points for each Excellent, 2 for each Satisfactory, 1 for every Needs to Improve, and 0 for every Poor. Total the points column and divide by 6 (the number of areas evaluated) for an overall assessment score.

Scoring Guide—Discussion

	Excellent (3 pt.)	Satisfactory (2 pt.)	Needs to Improve (1 pt.)	Poor (0 pt.)	Points
Reasoning	Frequently states issues and relevant information. Often elaborates with reasons, evidence, or explanations.	Sometimes states issues and relevant information. Sometimes elaborates with explanations, evidence, or reasons.	Rarely states issues or offers relevant information. Rarely elaborates with reasons, evidence, or explanations.	Does not state issue or offer relevant information. Does not elaborate.	
Speaking	Often offers valuable discussion contributions. Speaks clearly and confidently. Uses only appropriate language. Does not engage in personal attacks on others. Welcomes others' contributions.	Sometimes offers valuable discussion contributions. Speaks clearly. Uses only appropriate language. Does not engage in personal attack on others. Accepts others' contributions to discussion.	Sometimes contributes to discussion, but may try to discourage others from contributing to the discussion by monopolizing it. Sometimes does not speak clearly. Sometimes makes irrelevant or personal-attack statements.	Rarely contributes to discussion or interrupts others often. Does not speak clearly. Often makes irrelevant or personal-attack statements.	
Listening	Shows good consideration for others by listening carefully. Summarizes what another has said. Adds to another's statements. Asks relevant questions of speaker.	Displays some consideration for others by listening. Summarizes what another has said. Adds to another's statements. Asks relevant questions of speaker. May miss the point of what another has said.	Shows little consideration for others by listening carelessly. Occasionally summarizes what another has said, adds to another's statements, or asks relevant questions of speaker. Often misses the point.	Shows disregard for speakers; interrupts those who are speaking. Does not add to another's statements nor paraphrase another's ideas.	
				Total	

Overall Assessment Score: _____

Scoring Instructions: Score 3 points for each Excellent, 2 for each Satisfactory, 1 for every Needs to Improve, and 0 for every Poor. Total the points column and divide by 3 (the number of areas evaluated) for an overall assessment score.

Scoring Guide—Research Report

	Excellent (3 pt.)	Satisfactory (2 pt.)	Needs to Improve (1 pt.)	Poor (0 pt.)	Points
Research	Used at least 4 resources (videos, books, Web, encyclopedia, etc.), including at least one primary source.	Used at least 3 resources (videos, books, Web, encyclopedia, etc.), including at least one primary source.	Used just 2 secondary resources (videos, books, Web, encyclopedia, etc.) and no primary source.	Used only 1 secondary resource (video, book, Web, encyclopedia, etc.) and no primary source.	
Organization	Chose a topic in a timely manner. Developed at least 3 critical-thinking research questions. Met all project deadlines.	Chose a topic and developed 3 critical-thinking research questions. Met most project deadlines.	Had trouble picking a topic and developing 3 critical thinking research questions. Met at least one project deadline.	Had great difficulty choosing a topic, and had less than 3 critical thinking research questions. Did not meet deadlines.	
Report Content	Started with a strong lead. Presented information in a clear, orderly fashion. Report was accurate, engaging, and well thought-out.	Started with a good lead. Presented information in an orderly fashion. Mostly correct, interesting and well thought-out.	Followed a bland format instead of starting with a lead. Some parts of the report were unclear, had inaccuracies, or seemed hastily thrown together.	Poor or no lead. Showed little or no consideration of audience. Report was poorly written or inaccurate.	
Report Editing and Mechanics	Used active voice. Spelling, capitalization, grammar, punctuation, and sentence structure were correct.	Edited to reduce passive voice. Most spelling, capitalization, grammar, punctuation, and sentence structure were correct.	Rarely used active voice. Some spelling, capitalization, grammar, punctuation, and sentence structure were correct.	Did not attempt to use active voice. Many errors in spelling, capitalization, grammar, punctuation, and sentence structure.	
				Total	

Overall Assessment Score: _____

Scoring Instructions: Score 3 points for each Excellent, 2 for each Satisfactory, 1 for every Needs to Improve, and 0 for every Poor. Total the points column and divide by 4 (the number of areas evaluated) for an overall assessment score.

Scoring Guide—Presentation

	Excellent (3 pt.)	Satisfactory (2 pt.)	Needs to Improve (1 pt.)	Poor (0 pt.)	Points
Research	Use at least 4 resources (videos, books, Web, encyclopedia, etc.) including at least one primary source.	Used 3 resources (videos, books, Web, encyclopedia, etc.) including at least one primary source.	Used just 2 secondary resources (videos, books, Web, encyclopedia, etc.) and no primary source.	Used only 1 secondary resource (video, book, Web, encyclopedia, etc.) and no primary source.	
Delivery	Spoke loudly and clearly. Presentation lasted an appropriate length of time. Enthusiasm held audience's attention.	Spoke so that most could understand. Presentation was just a bit too long or short. Enthusiasm mostly held the audience's attention.	Spoke so that few people could understand. Presentation was too long or too short. Showed little enthusiasm, so audience's attention waned.	Whispered or mumbled. Presentation was way too short or way too long. Lack of enthusiasm caused audience to lose attention.	
Organization	Met all project deadlines; did not read aloud but referred to notes unobtrusively. Presented information in an orderly, logical fashion.	Met most project deadlines; did not read aloud but referred to notes unobtrusively. Presented information in an orderly fashion.	Met one project deadline; read aloud from notes or report or presented information in a haphazard fashion that was hard to follow.	Did not meet project deadlines; read aloud from notes or presented information in a manner that was difficult to follow.	
Materials	All materials were accurate and well thought out. Included at least one visual aid.	Most materials were accurate and well thought out. Included at least one visual aid.	Some materials had inaccuracies or were hastily thrown together. Did not include a visual aid.	Materials were poorly prepared or inaccurate. Did not include a visual aid.	
Audience	Considered audience when preparing. Made eye contact with audience and answered audience queries.	Showed some audience consideration. Made some eye contact with audience and tried to answer audience queries.	Showed little forethought for audience. Made infrequent eye contact with audience and did not make a strong effort to answer audience queries.	Did not think about the audience. Did not make eye contact, did not try to answer audience queries.	
				Total	

Overall Assessment Score: _____

Scoring Instructions: Score 3 points for each Excellent, 2 for each Satisfactory, 1 for every Needs to Improve, and 0 for every Poor. Total the points column and divide by 5 (the number of areas evaluated) for an overall assessment score.

Nonfiction Receptive Skills Checklist

Name _____   Date _____

A = almost always   **S = sometimes**   **N = not yet**

Respective Skills (Reading and Listening)	Rating
Reads grade-level nonfiction text independently.	
Previews texts to set a purpose for reading.	
Relates prior knowledge and experiences to understand and respond to new information.	
Makes, confirms, and revises predictions throughout the reading process.	
Monitors own comprehension while reading.	
Uses different strategies to tackle unknown words of difficult concepts.	
Creates mental images from pictures and print.	
Identifies the main idea and supporting details of expository text.	
Locates requested information in a passage.	
Recalls facts from what's been read.	
Knows the defining characteristics and text structures of nonfiction texts.	
Interprets maps, tables, and graphs included in passage.	
Makes inferences and draws conclusions based on explicit and implicit text information.	
Demonstrates an understanding of author's point of view.	
Shows critical and reflective thinking about the messages in text.	
Asks questions before, during, and after reading.	
Actively listens to nonfiction text.	
Visualizes what is being described.	
Distinguishes between fact and opinion in oral presentations.	
Discriminates between relevant and irrelevant data in oral presentations.	
Listens to classmates and adults.	
Listens in order to understand a speaker's topic, purpose, and perspective.	
Understands that an author's style, tone, and bias effect how the listener perceives the message.	
Identifies the speaker's viewpoint and possible motivation.	

Nonfiction Expressive Skills Checklist

Name_____   Date_____

A = almost always   **S = sometimes**   **N = not yet**

Expressive Skills (Speaking and Writing)	Rating
Makes contributions in class and group discussions.	
Responds to questions and comments.	
Conveys a clear main point when speaking to others and stays on topic.	
Asks questions of teachers and others.	
Plays a variety of roles in small group discussions.	
Retells sequential events in the correct order.	
Compares and contrasts information from several nonfiction texts.	
Reflects on what has been learned by formulating ideas, opinions, and personal responses to texts.	
Summarizes information effectively.	
Writes information in a logical order.	
Utilizes information-organizing strategies.	
Writes research papers.	

Research Skills	Rating
Identifies topics to investigate.	
Establishes questions to be answered by research.	
Gathers information about a topic using a variety of materials.	
Uses the part of the book and text structure to locate information.	
Uses graphic organizers to record information.	
Organizes information and ideas from multiple sources in a systematic way.	
Organizes ideas for oral presentations.	
Makes presentations in front of an audience.	

Self-Evaluation of Nonfiction Understanding

I'm good at _____

because _____

I'm improving at _____

because _____

I have trouble with _____

because _____

Self-Evaluation of Project, Report, or Presentation

The best part of my _____

was _____

because _____

I wish I had _____

because _____

Resources

Ausubel, D. (1978) "In Defense of Advanced Organizers: A Reply to the Critics." *Review of Educational Research*, 48, 251–257.

Bamford, R. and Kristo, J. (2000) *Checking Out Nonfiction K–8: Good Choices for Best Learning.* Christopher-Gordon Publishers, Inc.

Bean, T. and Bishop, A. (1992) "Polar Opposites: A Strategy for Guiding Students' Critical Reading and Discussion." in Dishner, E., Bean, T. and Readence, J. (1986) *Reading in the Content Areas: Improving Classroom Instruction.* (3rd Edition, pp. 247–254) Kendall/Hunt.

Beck, I. L., McKeown, M. G., Hamilton, R.L., and Kucan, L. (1997) *Questioning the Author: An Approach for Enhancing Student Engagement with Text*, International Reading Association.

Blachowicz, C. and Ogle, D. (2001) *Reading Comprehension: Strategies for Independent Learners*, The Guilford Press.

Bromley, K., Irwin-Devitis, L., and Modlo, M. (1999) *Fifty Graphic Organizers for Reading, Writing, and More.* Scholastic Professional Books.

Buehl, D. (2001) *Classroom Strategies for Interactive Learning*, International Reading Association.

Burns, P., Roe, B., and Ross, E. (1999) *Teaching Reading in Today's Elementary Schools*, Houghton Mifflin.

Capuzzi, D. (1973) "Information Intermix." *Journal of Reading*, 28, 684–689.

Castallo, R. (1976) "Listening Guides: A First Step Toward Notetaking and Listening Skills." *Journal of Reading*, 19, 289–290.

Crawley, S. and Mountain, L. (1995) *Strategies for Guiding Content Reading.* Allyn and Bacon.

Cunningham, D. and Shablack, S. (1975) "Selective Reading Guide-o-Rama: The Content Teacher's Best Friend," *Journal of Reading*, 18, 380–382.

Cunningham, J. (1982) "Generating Interactions Between Schemata and Text," in J. Niles and L. Harris (eds.) *New Inquiries in Reading Research and Instruction* (pp. 42–47). Thirty-first Yearbook of the National Reading Conference in Rochester, New York.

Cunningham, P. M., and Cunningham, J. W. (1987) "Content Area Reading-Writing Lessons." *The Reading Teacher*, 40, 506–512.

Davis, B. and Lass, B. (1996) *Elementary Reading Strategies That Work*, Allyn and Bacon.

Frayer, D., Frederick, W., and Klausmeier, H. (1969) *A Schema for Testing the Level of Concept Mastery.* Wisconsin Research and Development Center for Cognitive Learning.

Gambrell, L., Kapinus, B., and Wilson, R. (1987) "Using Mental Imagery and Summarization to Achieve Independence in Comprehension." *Journal of Reading*, 30, 638–642.

Gere, A., ed. (1985) *Roots in the Sawdust: Writing to Learn Across the Disciplines.* National Council of Teachers of English.

Harvey, S. (1998) *Nonfiction Matters: Reading, Writing, and Research in Grades 3–8.* Stenhouse Publishers.

Harvey, S. and Goudvis, A. (2000) *Strategies that Work.* Stenhouse Publishers.

Herber, H. (1978) *Teaching Reading in the Content Areas.* Prentice-Hall.

Resources *(cont.)*

Hoffman, J. (1992) "Critical Reading/Thinking Across the Curriculum: Using I-charts to Support Learning." *Lanugage Arts*, 69, 121–127.

Hunkins, F. (1995) *Teaching Thinking Through Effective Questioning.* Christopher-Gordon Publisher, Inc.

Johnson, D. and Pearson, P. D. (1984) *Teaching Reading Vocabulary*. Rinehart & Winston.

Joyce, B. and Weil, M. (1999) *Models of Teaching.* Prentice-Hall.

Keene, E. O. and Zimmermann, S. (1997) *Mosaic of Thought: Teaching Comprehension in a Reader's Workshop.* Heinemann.

King, A. (1991) "Effects of Training in Strategic Questioning on Children's Problem-solving Performance." *Journal of Educational Psychology*, 83, 307–317.

Klinger, J. and Vaughn, S. (1998) "Promoting Reading Comprehension, Content Learning and English Acquisition Through Collaborative Strategic Reading." *Reading Teacher*, 52, 738–747.

Klingner, J. K., and Vaughn, S. (1998) "Collaborative Strategic Reading: Involving All Students in Content Area Learning." *Teaching Exceptional Children*, 30, 323–337

Langrehr, J. (1988) *Teaching Students to Think.* National Educational Service.

Lyons, B. (1981) "The PQP Method of Responding to Writing." *English Journal*, 70, 42–43.

Manning, M. and Manning, G. (1996) "Teaching Reading and Writing: Speaking of Nonfiction." *Teaching Pre K–8*, 27, 108–109.

Manzo, A. (1969) "The ReQuest Procedure." *Journal of Reading*, 13, 123–126.

Manzo, A. and Casale, V. (1985) "Listen-read-discuss: A Content Reading Heuristic." *Journal of Reading*, 28, 732–734.

Manzo, A. and Manzo, U. (1997) *Content Area Literacy: Interactive Teaching for Interactive Learning.* Merrill.

Moore, D. W. and Moore, S. A. (1986) "Possible Sentences" in Dishner, E., Bean, T., and Readence, J. (1986) *Reading in the Content Areas: Improving Classroom Instruction.* Kendall/Hunt.

Moore, D. W., Moore, S. A., Cunningham, P. M., and Cunningham, J. W. (1998) *Developing Readers and Writers in the Content Areas K–12.* Longman.

Nagy, W. E. (1990) *Teaching Vocabulary to Improve Reading Comprehension.* International Reading Association.

Nichols, J. (1985) "The Content Reading-Writing Connection." *Journal of Reading*, 29, 265–267.

Ogle, D. (1986) "K-W-L: A Teaching Model that Develops Active Reading of Expository Text." *The Reading Teacher*, 39, 564–570.

Parker, W. (2001) *Social Studies in Elementary Education.* Prentice-Hall.

Raphael, T. E. (1984) "Question-answering Strategies for Children," *The Reading Teacher*, 36, 186–190.

Readance, J., Bean, T., and Baldwin, R. (2000) *Content Area Literacy: An Integrated Approach.* Kendall/Hunt.

Readence, J., Moore, D., and Rickelman, R. (2000) *Pre-reading Activities for Content Area Reading and Learning.* International Reading Association.

Resources *(cont.)*

Ricci, G. and Wahlgren, C. (1998) "The Key to Know 'PAINE' Know Gain." Paper presented at the 43rd Annual Convention of the International Reading Association, Orlando, Florida.

Robinson, F. (1961) *Effective Study.* Harper & Row.

Rose, L. (1989) *Picture This: Teaching Reading Through Visualization.* Zephyr Press.

Santa, C. (1988) *Content Reading Including Study Systems.* Kendall/Hunt.

Searfoss, L. and Readence, J. (2000) *Helping Children Learn to Read: Creating a Classroom Literacy Environment.* Allyn & Bacon.

Slavin, R. (1980) "Cooperative Learning," *Review of Educational Research*, 50, 315–342.

Standal, T. and Betza, R. (1990) *Content Area Reading: Teachers, Texts, and Students.* Prentice Hall.

Stauffer, R. G. (1969) *Directing Reading Maturity as a Cognitive Process.* Harper & Row.

Tierney, R., Readence, J., and Dishner, E. (1990) *Reading Strategies and Practices: A Compendium.* Allyn & Bacon.

Vacca, R. and Vacca, J. (1999) *Content Area Reading: Literacy and Learning Across the Curriculum.* Longman.

Vaughn, J. and Estes, T. (1986) *Reading and Reasoning Beyond the Primary Grades.* Allyn & Bacon.

Williams, D. (1986) "Unlocking the Question," in H. Carr's "Using Research to Support Teacher Change and Student Progress in Content Areas," Paper presented at the 31st annual convention of the International Reading Association in Philadelphia, Pennsylvania.

Wood, K., Lapp, D., and Flood, J. (1992) *Guiding Readers through Text: A Review of Study Guides.* International Reading Association.

Zarnowski, M. (1998) "Coming Out From Under the Spell of Stories: Critiquing Historical Narratives," *New Advocate*, 11, 345–356.

Zinsser, W. (1998) *On Writing Well: The Classic Guide to Writing Nonfiction.* HarperPerennial.